Haunted
London
Underground

HAUNTED
LONDON
UNDERGROUND

DAVID BRANDON & ALAN BROOKE

The
History
Press

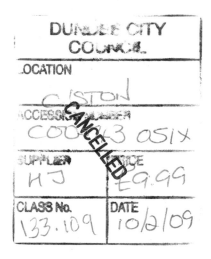
Frontispiece: Emergency stairs, Wapping. The brickwork dates from the original opening of the tunnel prior to being adapted for railway use. (© Pendar Sillwood)

First published 2008

The History Press Ltd
The Mill, Brimscombe Port
Stroud, Gloucestershire, GL5 2QG
www.thehistorypress.co.uk

© David Brandon & Alan Brooke 2008

British Library Cataloguing in Publication Data.
A catalogue record for this book is available from the British Library.

ISBN 978 0 7524 4746 9

Typesetting and origination by The History Press Ltd.
Printed in Great Britain

CONTENTS

Introduction   7

1   London and its Underground Railways   9

2   A Few Words about Ghosts   13

3   Haunted Underground Stations A to Z   17

4   Other Hauntings   73

5   Closed Railway Stations   77

6   Defunct Underground Stations   80

7   'Ghost' Steam Trains   82

8   The Haunted Underground in Film, Television and Books   88

INTRODUCTION

Anyone who has stood on a platform on the London Underground late at night will appreciate what an eerie place it can be. It has all the right conditions for a creepy, ghostly setting with its labyrinth of subterranean tunnels and passages and whatever might lurk down there. In addition there are the disused stations that were abandoned and now sport a haunting look. As a train speeds along passengers may catch a glimpse of one of the fabled 'ghost stations'. These have added to the fascination of the Underground with tales of what secrets may hide behind the sealed-off platforms, dusty tiles and crumbling staircases.

The Underground, which saw the Metropolitan Line open for business on 10 January 1863 with 30,000 passengers on the first day, is an engineering marvel. With over 270 stations and 253 miles of track carrying millions of people every year, the system is predictably crowded, claustrophobic and at times uncomfortable. Nonetheless it is a defining part of London's identity with its distinctive logo, map and architecture. In addition to serving the transport needs of the capital, it also served London during two wars when many Londoners sought refuge from enemy bombs. Not surprisingly it has inspired many stories, films as well as urban legends.

As it approaches its 150 years of history, the Underground has had its share of tragedies and deaths. Many burial grounds and plague pits have been disrupted as a consequence of extensions and developments. Staff working on the Underground at night have often reported strange incidents such as unexplained noises and sightings, feelings of unease and even encountering people who had reputedly died years earlier. This book will include a variety of stories including a faceless women, a 7ft figure, the ghosts of two actors, a woman in black, a thirteen-year-old girl who was murdered in the eighteenth century, reflections in carriage windows, screams of women and children who were crushed to death, semi-transparent apparitions, tales of troglodytes and even a screaming Egyptian mummy as well as other stories. Where possible we have attempted to explore the historical details behind some of these accounts. We believe there are many more stories to be told but is understandable that there is a reluctance by people to admit to having such experiences for fear of not being taken seriously or, worse, being ridiculed. What is particularly interesting is that many who have told of their experiences are or were sceptics when it came to believing in ghosts.

London has provided a rich seam for ghost stories and haunted places such as pubs, houses, lanes and various buildings. However, whilst accounts concerning the haunted Underground have found their way into ghost walks, Internet sites and general books about hauntings, there has been no specific book on the subject. We have also included a brief section on how the haunted Underground has been reflected in film and literature. Here then is a collection of spooky stories related to the London Underground with occasionally an item thrown in about other railway places with ghostly connections, even if they not part of the Underground system. Some of these stories are familiar; others have never appeared in print before. None belong entirely in the world of the fictional. Wherever possible the authors have included some historical material about the locations which they hope will help to put the events in their context and add to what the reader can gain from the book.

Particular thanks are expressed to the people who were kind enough to tell us of their personal experiences on the Underground. Acknowledgements also go to staff at the Guildhall Library, Oscar Butler for some of the photographs and Rod Corston for his unstinting help with organising the images.

1

LONDON AND ITS
UNDERGROUND RAILWAYS

London owes its very existence to possessing a geographical position largely favourable to transport. Given its size, it is not surprising that it has a very complex underground-railway system. Despite its infrastructure, fabric and rolling stock creaking at the seams from time to time and the fact that it has become a political football, it has for long played and continues to have an essential part in the social, economic and cultural life of London. 'Underground' is something of a misnomer. Only about 42 per cent of the system actually runs below the surface.

It could be argued that it isn't really a system at all in the strict sense of the word. In spite of the iconic nature of its logo, the station totem, the architectural merit of some of its buildings and the masterpiece of graphical design which is the Underground map, all giving a strong sense of system, the network grew up, at least until the early 1930s, in a largely piecemeal fashion. Many proposals for additional lines or extensions to existing ones have been mooted and then abandoned, never to see the light of day despite the likelihood that they were logical and would have made very useful contributions to the network. There are substantial parts of London that have never been well-served by the Underground network. Even with these reservations, the Underground is still a marvellous system. It is too easy to take it for granted; it is an essential part of the capital's infrastructure – life in London would be very different without it, and worse.

It is impossible to appreciate the history of modern London without some understanding of how and why the underground railway network developed. What follows is a brief chronological account of the growth of what, for convenience, we will call the 'system'. Some description and evaluation of the contribution that the system has made to London provides a useful background to the mysterious and often eerie events described in the main body of the book.

It may seem ironic to us in the twenty-first century that the London underground-railway network largely owes its origins to chronic road-traffic gridlock in the nineteenth century. It also results from the squalid living conditions endured by huge numbers of London's working people and the laudable desire to create a means of transport which would enable them to live in healthier districts just outside the central part of the Metropolis.

The first underground line to be built ran the four miles from Bishops Road at Paddington to Farringdon and was opened in 1863. It had the effect of relieving the traffic congestion on the New Road, London's first bypass. This is the permanent pandemonium of today's Marylebone, Euston and Pentonville Roads. Back in the nineteenth century, this road funnelled large amounts of traffic from the north and west of London heading particularly to the City and the Docks. The line formed the nucleus of the Metropolitan Railway and was built just below street level on what became known as the 'cut-and-cover' method. Wherever possible, the line was built in a cutting along and under existing roads and was then bricked over except for portions left open to the elements. This method may have caused temporary chaos for traffic but it reduced the potential costs involved in the compulsory purchase of many of the buildings that lay around the path of the projected route.

The trains were hauled by steam locomotives. The fact that the line was in a relatively shallow trench open to the air for much of the route enabled some of the smoke and steam to dissipate. However, the poisonous and almost impenetrable fug in stations such as Baker Street which were entirely subterranean, caused travellers to cough, splutter, expectorate and complain querulously while also providing a helpful environment for members of the light-fingered criminal fraternity. Early underground train travel was not for the faint-hearted.

An attempt was made to operate a locomotive that would tackle the pollution problem by being 'smokeless'. The idea was that a white-hot firebrick would heat the water in the locomotive's boiler and as a result produce steam for propulsion but no smoke. Robert Stephenson (1803-59) designed and built the experimental locomotive in 1861. This machine produced very little smoke but also very little steam and it was all it could do to haul itself around, let alone pull a train. It was regarded as a failure and quickly disappeared from public view. It gained the derisive nickname 'Fowler's Ghost' because no one was sure whether it actually existed or not.

In spite of apocalyptic predictions that the building of underground railways would disturb the Devil, who would then wreak his revenge in the ways that only he knew how, and equally dire warnings to the effect that tunnels and cuttings would collapse, the line from Paddington to Farringdon was an almost total success. So much so that there was soon talk of similar sub-surface cut-and-cover lines. One, a roughly circular route joining places of major importance, eventually became the Circle Line. Extensions were made to the Metropolitan Railway to reach Hammersmith in the west and the City in the east. Another line was the Metropolitan District which eventually reached out, far beyond the continuously built-up districts, to Wimbledon and Richmond in the south-west and Upminster in the east. The Metropolitan Railway had pretensions to being more than just a line serving London and its routes eventually extended deep into what were then almost entirely rural parts of Hertfordshire and Buckinghamshire before it effectively petered out in a field at the rustic spot of Brill, fifty or so miles from Baker Street. The East London line joined the inner part of the East End at Shoreditch with what became a mixed residential and industrial district around New Cross and New Cross Gate. It took over and used the tunnel under the Thames built by Marc and Isambard Kingdom Brunel. There had been many deaths during the building of this, the first significant underwater tunnel in the world.

In the central parts of the Metropolis, land values were too high to permit more cut-and-cover routes so attention turned to the building of deeper-level lines. There was already an extremely complex spaghetti of pipes, sewers and other services beneath the streets and it made sense to build below these. Crude technology was available in the form of the tunnelling shield invented by Marc Brunel for the Thames Tunnel. This was adapted to a circular form and used to build the first railway inside a tube. Opened in 1870, this line ran from Tower Hill to Bermondsey under the Thames and was cable operated. It was not very successful but Peter William Barlow modified the shield to build a line in a deep tube tunnel, also under the Thames. This was the City & South London Railway and it opened in

1890. Trains were powered by electricity. Later to become part of the Northern Line, the City & South London was hugely successful and it acted as the model for many other deep-level tube lines built over the next century. Improvements were made to Barlow's tunnelling shield by James Greathead (1844-1896) and modern tunnelling shields could be described as updates of Greathead's machine.

In spite of the fact that the early tube lines, such as the City & South London and the Central London Railway, provided an economic and efficient means of urban transport, it was left to a thrusting American entrepreneur, Charles Tyson Yerkes (1837-1905), to start creating a modern network in the 1900s. A number of lines had been built without any coordinated plan. Yerkes created the Underground Electric Railway Co., bringing these companies together, building short lines to join up the routes of some of the constituents, improving interchange facilities and creating an immediately recognisable brand: 'UndergrounD'.

In 1933 control of a unified underground system passed into the hands of the London Passenger Transport Board which set about a programme of extensions to the tube system and modernisation of rolling stock, stations and other facilities. It also created an immediately recognisable house style for the system, with close detail being paid to design issues as disparate as station architecture and the moquette used for seating. The deep-level tubes played a heroic role in the Second World War, sheltering vast numbers of Londoners during the Blitz with unused tubes acting as bomb-proof factories for war supplies and stores for valuable works of art. They also housed top-secret control centres having a major influence on the Allied war effort.

Since the war, new lines have been few and slow in coming but the Victoria Line, opened throughout in 1972 and the Jubilee Line Extension in 1999 have set new standards for automation. Controversially, maintenance of the infrastructure and rolling stock has passed into private hands. A common perception is that parts of the London Underground system are now creaking at the seams, run down and overcrowded for much of the time and comparing badly with similar systems in other major European cities. It is difficult not to see London's public transport system as a long-term pawn in party-political gamesmanship. It is perhaps a miracle that it works as well as it does.

Without question the London Underground has had an enormous social, economic and cultural impact on the Metropolis. Whatever its limitations, it has provided a ready means for people to get around quickly and easily, particularly in the central parts of London. It has acted to 'pull together' the remarkably disparate collection of 'villages' which constitutes London. It has stimulated and sometimes directly caused the growth of vast tracts of London's inner and more distant suburbia including, of course, the 'Metroland' affectionately mocked by Sir John Betjeman (1906-1984). It has assisted the regeneration of areas of inner-city decay as has been seen, for example, in the Bermondsey district of south-east London with the building of the Jubilee Line. It has given the world the immortal diagrammatic map of the system, originated by Harry Beck in 1932, a concept copied across the world. It has expressed itself in stations of the highest architectural merit such as Park Royal and East Finchley and the monumental headquarters block of No. 55 Broadway with its sculptures by Henry Moore and Jacob Epstein. More modestly it has given us the distinctive glazed terracotta station fronts, the colour of oxblood and the Art and Crafts faience work of the architect Leslie W. Green. These date from the 1900s and many of them can still be seen on the Bakerloo and the Piccadilly Lines, for example. London Transport and particularly the Underground have created a constant demand for advertising and poster art of the very highest quality.

Lest we get carried away with paeans of praise, it must be noted that there has been a price to pay for having the Underground. The building of the sub-surface lines was extraordinarily disruptive and often meant that people lost their homes, most frequently those who could not afford expensive legal counsel to contest compulsory purchase orders. Many burial sites had to be disturbed and human remains laid to rest elsewhere. Understandably this raised concerns among relatives and others that it should be done respectfully and reverentially. Perhaps it was inevitable that such episodes would lead to stories of ghosts, angry at this cavalier disruption of their repose, haunting the tunnels and stations built where the burial grounds had previously been. The underground railways have seen their share of murders and suicides and these have given rise to tales of consequent hauntings. Serious accidents have thankfully been few but again, probably inevitably, stories have developed that these events provoked a response from unexplained, possibly supernatural phenomena.

There are a sizeable number of closed underground stations. Can anyone with a soul honestly say that they do not experience at least some slight frisson of pleasurable terror at the idea of those cold, darkened tunnels and platforms and the thought of what might be lurking down there? It is difficult to think of many locations more suitable for hauntings and paranormal phenomena than underground stations, even working ones, especially at times when they are not open for public use. There are a few locations underground where it is possible to descry some fixtures such as the once shiny tiles on closed or relocated underground stations. It does not take much imagination to think that such stations come alive with their own residents during the hours when living travellers are at home and snug in their beds.

Many, especially of the deep-level tube stations, contain doors sealed off to access by the general public. What mysteries or possibly malevolent entities lurk behind these doors? Even many of the stations still in regular use are spooky first thing in the morning and last thing at night when few passengers are about and trains less frequent. Are the authors alone in being fascinated when travelling on the Underground on a Sunday as the train slows to pass through the platform of a station not open on that day of the week? The platform lights are dimmed and there seem to be minatory shadows a-plenty. What happens on the platforms and in the passages when no living entities are there?

2

A Few Words about Ghosts

The ultimate mystery of life is what happens to us when we die. Is the vital spark, the soul that makes us distinctive individuals, simply snuffed out only to be followed immediately by the decay of our physical parts? Most of us are uncomfortable with the idea that the world with which we are so familiar continues after we have died. How much better it is to hope or believe that something awaits us; that there is indeed an afterlife. Such a possibility, however, is viewed by most of us with a mixture of fascination and trepidation.

We love mysteries and phenomena that we cannot explain. This is evident by the huge amount of films, books, television programmes, ghost walks and themed places such as the London Dungeon that caters for such interests. Ghosts, it seems, remain as much a part of our culture as they did in the medieval period although our understanding and relationship with the idea has changed. They are part of the rich tapestry of folklore and legend as well as the subject of serious academic study – or at least our desire to want to believe in them (see for example the excellent analysis by Owen Davies, *The Haunted, A Social History of Ghosts*, Palgrave 2007).

Traditionally hauntings have been associated with locations that lend themselves to the presence of ghostly experiences such as old houses, graveyards, and historic buildings. These locations usually build on stories related with the death of someone – often violent such as a murder or suicide. London in particular has a rich history of haunted places. However, no book has been published dedicated to hauntings on the London Underground. This is surprising, given the eerie atmosphere of the system with its tunnels, disused stations and close proximity to burial sites and plague pits. The Underground has also witnessed a great deal of human tragedy with many deaths resulting from accident, murder and suicide.

There are many distinctions to be made when dealing with the subject matter of hauntings and unexplained phenomena. Ghosts and hauntings take many forms. A particular place can be haunted not only by a ghost but also by other supernatural phenomena. For this reason this section will briefly outline a variety of manifestations. The reader will find more comprehensive definitions in the many encyclopaedias on ghosts, spirits and the supernatural, such as *Chambers Dictionary of the Unexplained* (2007) or *The Encyclopaedia of Ghosts and Spirits* by Rosemary Guiley (2000).

Most religions have created destinations for the souls of the departed. In the case of Christianity, this is Heaven, the place for the good where arrivals can expect to enjoy a perpetual idyllic existence; and Hell, a state of continuous torment for those who have given themselves over to a life of sin. Some Christians believe in the older idea of Purgatory, a place where souls have to endure various trials and tribulations until they are judged whether they deserve to proceed to Heaven.

If it is thought that our souls live on in another world, then it is only a small step to visualise the dead returning to the living world. Ghosts have fascinated and frightened mankind for thousand of years. They have certainly captured the imagination of the British and given rise to the plethora of allegedly haunted sites throughout the country.

There are many ways in which ghosts manifest themselves. They may be seen or heard. People have claimed to 'sense' the presence or activity of a ghost either through smell or a fall in temperature. Many witnesses admit to not believing in ghosts but at the same time have experienced some strange phenomena. These people may sometimes be reluctant to report their experience for fear of ridicule, hence their stories go unrecorded.

The nearest anyone has come to capturing a ghost is on film but the authenticity of such images has often been disputed. Rarely has more than one person seen a ghost at the same time. But why should ghosts want to haunt the living? Many views have been offered. Some people argue that the souls of the dead cannot rest because of the terrible or tragic way in which they ended their lives. These of course include murder or suicide.

In the medieval period accounts of ghosts were regularly told and it was important that the Church conveyed certain messages about the sacraments, the forgiveness for sins and the ways in which the living might assist the dead through prayers, Masses and alms giving. The Catholic Church taught that ghosts were the souls of those trapped in Purgatory (a halfway stage after death between earth and Heaven), unable to rest until they had suffered for their sins. Many religions going as far back as ancient Egypt believed that dead were obliged to undergo judgement.

Before the nineteenth century it was usual for people to want to banish ghosts by various means such as exorcisms. However from the nineteenth century a change in attitude towards ghosts occurred. With the rise of spiritualism and the growth of mediums it became more fashionable to want to contact the dead. Rather than make a spirit materialise, mediums attempted to transmit messages from the dead to the family or friends. Concerned with the number of charlatans and those preying on people suffering from bereavement (and also prompted by the imprisonment of Helen Duncan in the 1940s on charges of witchcraft), the government introduced the Fraudulent Mediums Act of 1951, which repealed the Witchcraft Act of 1735. Its declared intent was to punish persons who 'fraudulently purport to act as spiritualistic mediums or to exercise powers of telepathy, clairvoyance or other similar powers.'

A dictionary usually defines a ghost as the soul of a dead person, a disembodied spirit wandering among or haunting living persons. Variations on this view suggest that a ghost represents the energy, soul or personality of a person who has died and has become lost or stuck between this plane of existence and the next. Because they are lost they are not aware that they are dead. Sceptics argue that experiences of hauntings and ghosts are the products of our own minds. We see ghosts because we want to see them.

The word 'ghost' has a variety of associations including apparition, phantom, wraith, revenant, poltergeist, spook, spectre and spirit. A spirit is defined as a supernatural being or essence which can come in a multitude of guises. It is often a malevolent being that is bodiless but can become visible and also enter and possess a human being.

An 'apparition' is the supernatural appearance of a person – dead or living, animal or inanimate object. Apparitions only appear briefly and tend to disappear very quickly. Most experiences of an apparition involve hearing, smelling or feeling as much as seeing. They can move through walls, cast shadows or be reflected in a mirror. Most manifestations are associated with communicating a message or giving a warning to the living. Some explanations for their sightings suggest they may be visual hallucinations. A *crisis apparition* is usually a vision of a person that appears before a recipient. The vision is usually a person who is undergoing some form of crisis such as a serious illness, an injury or even death. The recipient learns at a later stage that the person has died. These eerie cases have some conviction about them largely because the person who saw the vision tells someone else before any confirmation of the death. A similar definition is that of a' wraith' which is also the apparition of a living person and it appears as a portent just before a person's death or at the moment of death. Such experiences are similar to the type of dreams that have an uncanny habit of actually happening shortly after. The term 'phantom' has similar characteristics to an apparition although phantoms are sometimes feared.

A 'revenant' is the spirit of a person who returns after a lengthy absence. Revenants also demonstrate the belief that if the dead are not buried properly, they will not be able to find their way into the 'other world' or might even be barred from entering it. Such a state, it was believed, led the spirit to wander between the world of the living and the world of the dead in search of their resting place. These lost souls might turn their anger against the living who failed to provide them with the proper passage to the next world. Revenants were usually thought of as people who used to be wrongdoers when they were alive – wicked, vain or unbelievers. They were associated with spreading disease and the only way to be rid of them was exhumation followed by decapitation, burning or removal of the heart.

A 'poltergeist' is a ghost or spirit which manifests its presence by noises and knockings. Poltergeists are also blamed for hiding possessions, throwing things across rooms or even pulling people's clothing or hair or scratching them. They are defined as a mischievous demon or spirit and can generate very real fear. These small grotesque supernatural creatures usually make trouble for human beings and in medieval times were associated with the Devil.

Other unexplained phenomena include ghost lights or orbs – mysterious lights usually seen as white or blue balls or yellow spheres. There have been reports of these as well as some photographs allegedly showing them in the London Underground. Sightings of orbs evolved mainly with the advent of digital cameras in the 1990s and there is some scepticism about what they actually represent. Advocates of them have suggested there is a link between suicides or violent deaths and the sighting of an orb.

What other notable features are associated with ghosts? Well, we nearly always think of hauntings taking place at night or in the dark – these are much more common than daytime experiences. To this extent the Underground is particularly well-placed for unexplained phenomena.

Their presence will continue to haunt a building even when that structure has been demolished and replaced by another. Ghosts are often seen as grey or white rather than in black although the shadow of them might give that impression. In the medieval period it was believed that when a soul passed through Purgatory it changed from black to white. Ghosts, like vampires, demons and witches for that matter, cannot cross running water.

Is there a limited duration of life for ghosts, or put another way, how long do ghosts exist? It is rare for ghosts of Iron Age, Bronze Age, Stone Age and prehistoric people to be documented. A general view is that spirits make a one-off appearance shortly after their death to people close to them in order to bring messages of comfort. Yet there are those that persist in haunting a particular place for years. We often hear of a ghost from a period hundreds of years ago whose presence continues to haunt a house. However, the persistence of such stories may be more to do with the transmission of collective storytelling through time.

Finally, can inanimate objects such as trains, coaches or clothing take on a ghost-like appearance? After all, such objects do not possess consciousness and were never 'alive'. This has proved to be something of a conundrum and has been discussed over many years. Why should a ghost choose to wear particular types of clothing? Although many people were buried in shrouds ghosts are often seen wearing everyday clothing. It is rare to see a ghost in the 'all together'. The afterlife would be a very cluttered place if items of clothing as well as untold other types of objects resided there. One explanation suggests that inanimate objects are mirages or pre-recorded impressions of some kind, rather than actual manifestations. Other explanations hold that ghosts have the ability to represent to the viewer whatever they want to see and that clothes are an important item of identity, especially when it comes to recognising a ghost from a particular period in the past.

This book is not concerned with proving or disproving the reality of ghosts. As social and cultural historians we are interested in all manifestations of popular culture and want to record, analyse and attempt to explain their significance. It is not necessary as historians that we should believe or disbelieve in ghosts. There are many reports that more than stretch the imagination of a believer whilst other accounts are sincere, believable and difficult to explain. It is up to the reader to draw his or her own conclusions but we hope that readers will agree that the Underground provides one of the best locations to interest both believers and sceptics.

3

HAUNTED UNDERGROUND
STATIONS A TO Z

ALDGATE

Aldgate Station is on the Circle Line between Tower Hill and Liverpool Street, as well as being the
eastern terminus of the Metropolitan Line. The station, which dates back to 1876, has some notable
associations. In addition to the ghost of an old woman, it features in one of the Sherlock Holmes
stories, *The Bruce-Partington Plans*, where Holmes becomes involved in solving the mystery of a
dead body which had struck the lines just before the train reached the station. In September 1888
the body of Ripper victim Catherine Eddowes was murdered nearby in Mitre Square, Aldgate. Not
surprisingly the station provides the starting point for the popular 'Jack the Ripper' walks.

The area has a long history and was the easternmost gateway through the London Wall from the
City of London. Aldgate Station has suffered bombing and tragedy. It was badly damaged by German
bombing during the Second World War, and in July 2005 one of the four bombs in the London
suicide bombings exploded on a Circle Line train as it left Liverpool Street and was approaching
Aldgate Station, killing seven innocent people and inflicting awful injuries on others.

With its open-air platforms it may seem a less likely location for ghostly sightings than a deeper
level station. However, given the rich history of the area it would be surprising if the ghosts of
the past did not cast their presence there in some way or other. Aldgate Station is built almost on
the site of one of the biggest plague pits in London. Next door to the station stands St Botolph's
Church where over 1,000 plague victims were buried in the graveyard in the space of two weeks
in September 1665. In *A Journal of the Plague Year* Daniel Defoe described the horrors of death at
Aldgate:

> I went all the first part of the time freely about the streets, though not so freely as to run myself into
> apparent danger, except when they dug the great pit in the churchyard of our parish of Aldgate. A
> terrible pit it was, and I could not resist my curiosity to go and see it. As near as I may judge, it was
> about forty feet in length, and about fifteen or sixteen feet broad, and at the time I first looked at it,
> about nine feet deep; but it was said they dug it near twenty feet deep afterwards in one part of it …
> Into these pits they had put perhaps fifty or sixty bodies each; then they made larger holes wherein
> they buried all that the cart brought in a week … At the beginning of September, the plague raging

Catherine Eddowes was the fourth of five confirmed Ripper victims. This sign marks the place near to where she was murdered in Mitre Square, close to Aldgate Station.

Catherine Eddowes was found lying in a dark corner at Mitre Square.

Aldgate Station opened in 1876.

in a dreadful manner, and the number of burials in our parish increasing to more than was ever buried in any parish about London … they ordered this dreadful gulf to be dug – for such it was, rather than a pit …the pit being finished the 4th of September, I think, they began to bury in it the 6th, and by the 20th, which was just two weeks, they had thrown into it 1,114 bodies when they were obliged to fill it up.

Deaths from plague in Aldgate exceeded 4,000. In the history of excavation of the Underground the disturbance of bodies from old burial sites during excavation is not uncommon. Given London's huge population over the centuries it is not surprising that burial sites have been found located near Underground stations or tunnels. During redevelopment in 2005 by the Museum of London Archaeology Service (MoLAS) a number of burials were uncovered relating to the Aldgate burial ground. The majority of bodies were interred in wooden coffins with some showing traces of name plates. A total of 238 burials were recorded with several bodies having been truncated by nineteenth- and twentieth-century construction. MoLAS suggested that as some of the graves contained the remains of more than two individuals (four or five in some cases) it was possible that internment was the result of plague.

Aldgate Station has been associated with a great deal of unexplained activity involving unusual noises and sightings. So frequent yet so strange are these sightings that they have reputedly been recorded in the station log. A well-known story concerns a track worker who was working a late

St Botolph's Church, which stands next door to Aldgate Station, was the site of a mass plague pit.

shift at the station a few years ago. The man suddenly slipped as he bent over the rails and came into contact with the 20,000 volt conductor rail which caused a massive surge of electricity to pass through his body. The shock knocked him unconscious and he was fortunate not to be killed. Remarkably he survived, albeit with some general bruising. One of his co-workers working nearby witnessed the incident but also saw a most eerie sight. Just seconds before the man touched the live rail, his colleague saw the figure of half-transparent old woman gently stroking the man's hair. The old woman was believed to have been killed during the Second World War by falling onto a similar rail.

Other strange stories have been associated with the station. Apart from many unexplained sightings, passengers have reported the sound of footsteps in the early hours of the morning approaching them, then fading away into the distance, but there has been no visible sign of anyone being around to produce footsteps. Strange and mournful whistling has been reported although this is an occurrence experienced on other Underground stations.

One explanation for this has been the extent of infrasound. Infrasound is sound with a frequency too low to be heard by human ear and has been often used to monitor earthquakes. It is known to cause feelings of sickness but as it is not consciously perceived, it can make people feel that they are experiencing supernatural events. Vic Tandy and Tony Lawrence of the psychology department at Coventry University wrote a paper called 'Ghosts in the Machine' for the journal of the *Society for Psychical Research*. In this they cited infrasound as the cause of apparitions seen by staff at a so-called haunted laboratory in Warwick. Tandy appeared on the Channel 5 programme, *Ghosts on the Underground* (2006), in order to detect similar phenomena at London Underground stations where high levels of supernatural activity had been recorded. Escalator motors, moving trains or wind from the tunnels can produce distorted sounds, particularly on deep-level tube stations although Aldgate has open-air platforms.

ALDWYCH

Of all the London Underground stations, Aldwych can claim some fame with regard to hauntings. It is a disused station and therefore could itself be described as a ghost station; it has had a number of ghost sightings and it has also become the location for television and film productions (see the section on Film and Television) as well as a museum piece. Films shot at Aldwych Underground Station include: *Death Line* (1972); *Ghost Story* (1973); *The Krays* (1990); *Patriot Games* (1992); the horror film *Creep* (2004); *V for Vendetta* (2006); and *Atonement* (2007). The station is even included in the video game *Tomb Raider 3*. In 2002 it had a whole programme, *Most Haunted*, dedicated to investigating the ghosts allegedly found there.

Aldwych was formerly on the Piccadilly Line and was the terminus of a short branch from Holborn until it was closed in September 1994. Situated on the Strand and surrounded by the buildings of King's College, London University, it was opened as the Strand Station in November 1907 running a shuttle service to Holborn, with a single late-night service running through to Finsbury Park for the use of theatre-goers. The station was built on the site of the Royal Strand Theatre, and this is relevant to the station's hauntings as one of the ghosts associated with the theatre has been seen lurking around the station platform. The station changed its name to Aldwych in 1917.

During the war the branch was closed with the operational platform being used as a public air-raid shelter, and the disused platform and running tunnel used to house some of the valuable artefacts from the British Museum including the Elgin Marbles. In the 1970s when the Fleet Line was being planned (later the Jubilee Line) it was intended that it would run from Charing Cross via Aldwych to Ludgate Circus and on to east London. Although the plan did not come to fruition, a few hundred yards of experimental tunnel was dug from Charing Cross to Aldwych. This still exists but was of course never used. Despite being out of use for a number of years, Aldwych Station has a well-preserved interior. It has two entrances – one on the Strand and another around the corner on Surrey Street. The exterior was designed by Leslie Green (1875-1908), the English architect known for his iconic glazed-terracotta facades on a number of London Underground stations during the first decade of the twentieth century.

Between the end of the nineteenth century and 1914 a major redevelopment took place in the Strand district. Slums that had occupied the area between Drury Lane and Lincoln's Inn Fields were demolished, several streets were destroyed and the two new thoroughfares of Kingsway and Aldwych were built in their place. The rebuilding wiped out a slice of Victorian theatre history, including the Royal Strand Theatre which was bought out by the railway company and made way for Aldwych Station. The theatre, which was decorated in white, gold and silver, was described by *Punch* magazine in 1841 as 'this elegant little theatre'. It changed is name to Punch's Playhouse in 1850 but reverted to being called the Royal Strand Theatre in 1858. In 1882 the theatre closed for extensive reconstruction mainly to improve access to and from the auditorium. The most successful show to be staged there was the

Aldwych Station, Strand entrance. The station is the main Underground location for films and television programmes.

record-breaking musical comedy, *The Chinese Honeymoon*, which opened in October 1901 and ran for 1,075 performances until 1904. The theatre closed on 13 May 1905 to make way for the construction of the station, with the last performance, a musical, running for a few performances only from 5 May.

One rumour suggests that the ghost of an actress who believes she has not enjoyed her last curtain call walks the station. Workers on the Underground have reported a number of sightings. 'Fluffers' were people who used to clean the accumulation of dust from the tunnels of the Underground network, particularly the human hair and skin cells that were shed by the 3 million daily passengers. Since the 1970s they have been replaced by the five-car Tunnel Cleaning Train which clears the debris. At Aldwych many 'fluffers' reported being scared by a figure who appeared on the tracks at night. When it was mooted that the theatre was to close a number of actresses were very angry and protested. There certainly would be a number of contenders for the ghost of an actress. The last performance there, a musical by Howard Talbot called *Miss Wingrove*, might well have had aggrieved any one of the female cast who found the play closing down after a week. An interesting history of the theatre and the building of the station is offered by Paul Hadley, 'From Stage to Platform: The Metamorphosis of the Strand Theatre 1830-1905', in *London Passenger Transport* 1984 No. 12 April, pp 588-593.

In over seventy years many actresses, both well known and lesser known, performed at the theatre. Notable names included Mary Anne Keeley (1806-1899), Louisa Cranstoun Nisbett (1812-1858), Mrs Stirling – Lady Fanny Gregory (1817-1895), Marie Wilton – later Lady Bancroft (1839-1921), Ethel

Aldwych Station, Surrey Street entrance.

Irving (1869-1963), Priscilla Horton (1818-1895), Violet Vanburgh (1856-1942), Ada Swanborough (1845-1893 – the manager's daughter who for some strange reason was brought up as a boy until the age of sixteen), and Frances Raymond who committed suicide in the US by inhaling gas in 1901. The *New York Times* described Frances Raymond as 'demented'.

Can any further light be cast on whom the ghost might be? When the television series *Most Haunted* chose to investigate Aldwych Station in 2002 for any ghostly activity they came a little closer to experiencing the presence of the actress but no closer to saying which one. Armed with a fifteen-strong camera crew, medium Derek Achorah and ex-*Blue Peter* presenter Yvette Fielding spent a day walking the tunnels in complete darkness as well as attempting to pick up signs of supernatural activity from the platform.

Acknowledging that there had been many sightings of a young actress, the team proceeded to enter the tunnels. A site manager said that it was natural to be very nervous working in the empty stations as strange noises from trains, the wind and inexplicable factors heightened the tensions. He also admitted that Aldwych did have a particular level of paranormal activity. The eastern tunnel, which closed within ten years of the station opening, is the one that has created eerie feelings and sightings. Achorah said he felt the presence of two females and one male although there appeared to be some confusion with one of the females and the man. The female, whose suggested name was Alice Humphrey, was described as touching the head of a man before he was electrocuted on the line – the same story as Aldgate. This was then qualified by saying that the man had also worked at

The scary approach to the haunted platform on Aldwych Station. (© Hywell Williams, whose excellent website is http://underground-history.co.uk/front.php.)

Aldwych as well as Aldgate – but back to our actress. The name Margaret was mentioned with a possible middle name or other name of Estelle and a surname sounding like Bryce or Bright.

During the filming noises were detected, shadows in tunnels were sighted and strange orb-like lights – which usually signal the arrival of a manifestation – came out on the photography. Parapsychologist Jason Karl confessed to feeling more disturbed at Aldwych Station's platform and tunnels than anywhere else he had ever been and had no desire to go back.

Despite this investigation the identity of the actress is still not known and can only be speculated at. Harriet Waylett (1798-1851) was the sole owner of the theatre in 1834. Errol Sherson, in *London's Lost Nineteenth Century Theatres* (1925), said that although Waylett was a singer of some repute she was also a drunkard who had a very bad temper. Frances 'Fanny' Kelly (1790-1882) opened at the Strand in February 1833 in which she was advertised as playing twenty different characters. We might consider that some descriptions of the Aldwych ghost said she appeared in many guises! Although Fanny Kelly was successful elsewhere, Sherson states that she failed at the Strand. Ada Cavendish (1839-1895) left instructions for her jugular vein to be severed before burial – not an uncommon request amongst people who feared premature burial. No actress seems to appear with the name Margaret or the surname Bryce or Bright. Possibly the ghost was a lesser-known figure who never quite made a career on stage but who looks desperately for applause or that elusive last curtain call.

BANK

Beneath the streets of the City there is a vast underground tunnel that links Bank Station and Monument Station, running the length of King William Street. Whilst the stations are officially known as the Bank-Monument complex they retain separate identities, platforms and entrances. Many commuters familiar with Bank Station will know that there is a longish walk involved between the stations. Bank-Monument is one of the largest and most complex subterranean railway stations in the world. The station, which is named after the nearby Bank of England on Threadneedle Street, was opened in 1900 for the Central London Railway, whilst Monument Station had been completed

Bank Station. One of the entrances is located next to the Bank of England.

for the (Inner) Circle Line in 1884 about 100yds away. Faced with the expense of building in a prime property area of London, the City and South London Railway (later part of the Northern Line) tried to save on costs by cutting beneath St Mary Woolnoth Church to build the lift shafts and station. After much objection the railway company bought the crypt for what is now the Northern Line booking hall so the entrance that once led to the crypt now leads into Bank Underground Station. In 1982 as the station was closing a worker who was walking across the ticket hall heard a banging coming from inside the lift, despite the fact that he just checked it and there was no one else around.

As with many examples involved in the construction and extension of the Underground, burial sites have been disturbed. In this case the bones of the dead were moved for reburial at the City of London Cemetery, Ilford, in 1900.

During the Blitz, Bank Station received a direct hit by a bomb in January 1941 which penetrated the road surface and exploded in an escalator machinery room, killing fifty-six people and injuring sixty-nine. In 1960 Bank Underground Station opened Europe's first 'travelator' – a 300-ft moving walkway. The terminal for the Docklands Light Railway was built beneath the Northern Line platforms in 1991 and it was then that the whole complex became known unofficially as Bank-Monument.

Although, as yet, there have been no reports of any of the disturbed souls that were moved in 1900 there has been the sighting of a ghost that has become associated with the station as well as the nearby Bank of England. The ghost is reputed to be that of Sarah Whitehead who has gained the nickname of the 'Bank Nun' (or in some cases the 'Black Nun'). Workmen building that part of the Underground first saw her ghostly apparition at Bank Station in the late nineteenth century. On another occasion a worker chased what he thought was an old lady locked in the station during the early hours of the

The Bank of England. A little further down Threadneedle Street is the Bank of England Museum where an illustration of Sarah Whitehead, the 'Bank Nun', is on display.

morning. When he thought he had caught her up she disappeared down a corridor with no possible exit. Some years later an employee reported seeing a female figure who suddenly disappeared. This was particularly disturbing as the station was closed and no member of the public should have been there. There have been further reports down to recent times of the ghost of Sarah desperately searching for something or somebody. Why does Sarah wander the area and why is she called the Bank Nun?

Our story goes back to 1811 when Sarah's brother was charged with forgery and brought before the Old Bailey to stand trial. Her brother, Philip Whitehead, who is referred to as Paul at the trial on 30 October 1811, was a former employee at the Bank of England. A transcript of the trial can be viewed on the excellent Old Bailey online website (http://www.hrionline.ac.uk/oldbailey/).

Paul Whithead was indicted on the first account of 'feloniously forging and counterfeiting … a certain bill of exchange' for over £87. Five other counts of forgery followed. The law took a very grave view of forgery and it was a crime for which there was no pardon. Six months earlier two employees at the Bank of England, Richard Armitage and C. Thomas, had been executed at Newgate.

They too had appeared at the Old Bailey and were found guilty of forgery. At their trial it was said that there was alarm at the 'many forgeries which for some time had been practised on the Bank of England and the commercial part of the metropolis.' Given the extent of forgery it was not surprising that there was a great deal of sensitivity to the issue by the time Paul Whitehead took the stand.

Whitehead had worked as a clerk in the cashier's office at the Bank of England but had resigned from his job on 2 August 1810. The crimes for which he was charged were against a number of businessmen and not the Bank itself. One of those testifying against Whitehead described him as 'a respectable man'. Whether his leaving the Bank motivated his move into forgery or whether he had been guilty of the offence whilst at the Bank, we do not know. It has been speculated that he lived a lifestyle that he found difficult to pay for and so resorted to forgery. At his trial Paul left his defence to his counsel and he called upon one witness who gave him a good character reference. It proved to be in vain and, at the age of thirty-six, Paul Whitehead was sentenced to death.

Whilst the trail and subsequent execution had been going on, his devoted sister, Sarah, had been taken to a house in Fleet Street and protected from all news of her brother. Anxious to find out about his whereabouts she set off to the Bank of England in search of him. She asked a clerk who, presumably not knowing who she was, blurted out that her brother had received the death sentence for the said crimes. Stunned and shocked by this news, Sarah could not come to terms with what she had been told and it clearly affected her mind. Shortly after she took to visiting the Bank on a regular basis dressed in black-crepe veil and long dress still asking for her brother. The staff nicknamed her the Bank Nun after her appearance but her visits became a source of pity as well as a nuisance to the Bank.

At first the Bank even offered to compensate her for her suffering and loss. Poor Sarah then convinced herself that the Bank was conspiring against her. The bank eventually lost patience with Sarah's continual visits and six years after the death of her brother they tried to come an agreement with her. The arrangement was that they would pay her a sum of money if she agreed not to visit the Bank, which she accepted. Clearly Sarah was not too grief stricken and confused to accept this. Sarah visited the bank and loitered near the entrance between 1812-1837 attired in heavy mourning dress which contrasted strangely with her painted cheeks. After she died Sarah has been seen dressed in black, even on the platforms of

The famous London Underground logo showing Bank Station.

Sarah Whitehead, the 'Bank Nun'. This image appears by kind permission of the Governor and Company of the Bank of England. The original can be seen in the Bank of England Museum.

the station, still searching and asking, 'has anyone seen my brother?' Sarah was reputedly buried in the old churchyard of St Christopher-le-Stocks, which afterwards became part of the Bank's gardens.

If Sarah was buried at St Christopher-le-Stocks then she would have been in the company of another ghost, William Jenkins, who died at the age of thirty-one in March 1798. His tall figure has been sighted on a number of occasions around the area. In August 1933 when excavations were carried out in relation to the rebuilding of the Bank a lead coffin, measuring 7ft 6in, was discovered beneath the old Garden Court which had once been the churchyard of St Christopher-le-Stocks. Jenkins, a former clerk at the Bank, had been 6ft 7½in in height. He feared that his corpse would be stolen by body snatchers and asked permission from the directors of the Bank to bury it in the Bank's Garden Court. His request was granted and Jenkins was buried very early one morning before business began. In July 1923 an Act of Parliament provided that any human remains removed from the site of the former churchyard of St Christopher's should be re-interred at Nunhead Cemetery (near Peckham) or any other consecrated burial ground.

Some accounts suggest that the nickname of the Bank of England, 'The Old Lady of Threadneedle Street,' is a reference to Sarah. This is not the case. The Bank of England Museum states that the first mention of the nickname appeared in print as the caption *Political Ravishment or The Old Lady of Threadneedle Street in danger,* to a cartoon published in 1797 by James Gillray. The cartoon depicts William Pitt the Younger, the Prime Minister, 'pretending to woo the Bank, which is personified by an elderly lady wearing a dress of £1 notes seated on a chest of gold.'

BECONTREE

Becontree Station is one of many Underground stations where there has been at least one sighting of a ghost. Frustratingly, sightings at stations in general have been acknowledged but as we have mentioned before there is an understandable reluctance for those who have such experiences to make them public. Becontree Station is located towards the east end of the District Line and was opened in 1932.

The reported haunting by a station employee in 1992 concerns the sighting of a faceless woman with blonde hair standing on the platform. As with so many sightings this was experienced during the hours when the station was closed and therefore few people were present. The sighting of the apparition was preceded by the sound of knocking on the office doors. Needless to say the employee was scared out of his skin. There has been at least one further sighting of the woman although it is still unclear as to her identity. The *Encyclopaedia of Ghosts and Spirits* (R. Guiley) explains that sightings of faceless women appear in haunting legends around the world: 'The ghost is a beautiful woman usually seen first from behind, who terrifies people when they discover she has no face.'

BETHNAL GREEN STATION

Bethnal Green Station was the scene of the worst civilian disaster of the Second World War as well as being the largest loss of life in a single incident on the London Underground. The station is on the Central Line between Liverpool Street and Mile End Stations. It was part of the 'New Works Programme 1935-1940' to coordinate underground trains, tram, trolleybus and bus services in the capital and surrounding areas and was used as an air-raid shelter during the war.

From the nineteenth century Bethnal Green had a reputation for being a working-class area, suffering the deprivations of poor housing and unsanitary conditions which made it one of the poorest slums in London. In October 1863 *The Illustrated London News* reported on the 'condition of the poorer neighbourhoods of Bethnal Green' and drew attention to deaths caused by blood poisoning, 'through the impure state of the dwellings'. It added that a 'wide and populous district has for years been subject to all the foulest influences which accompany a state of extreme filth and squalor which may be due to the fact that private moneyed interests have had little to fear from parochial authority.'

The East End of London had experienced heavy bombing raids during the war but, on 3 March 1943, 173 people (twenty-seven men, eighty-four women and sixty-two children) were killed and ninety-two were injured in a crush whilst attempting to enter the station. Two days before British bombing raids on Berlin had brought some optimism on the part of those on the receiving end of the Luftwaffe's attentions but it also brought an expectation of retaliation. As the siren sounded at 8.17 p.m., hundreds of people ran from the darkened streets to Bethnal Green Tube Station where some 500 people were already sheltering. Within minutes 1,500 people had entered the shelter. Ten minutes later loud noises outside panicked many who were entering the station and there was pushing, shoving and then a surge forward. Adding to the panic was the narrow entrance to the station, a dimly lit staircase and wetness caused by rain during the day. As a woman near the bottom of the staircase slipped, others fell over and within seconds over 300 men, women and children were crushed into the tiny stairwell. People were terrified and panicking as they fell over with many more trying to push their way into the shelter. The rescuers found it almost impossible to help. Eyewitness accounts described the awful 'screaming and hollering' as people were 'piled up like sardines.'

Questions have always surrounded the tragedy. The incident was not reported at the time because of government censorship, which omitted the precise location, and so the disaster did not attract great public sympathy for the victims and survivors. It seemed that all traces of the event had been covered over, which in turn led to rumour and speculation. It was not until 1946 that a report was finally released and the verdict was that the tragedy had been caused by panic made worse by the narrow entrance to the shelter, poor lighting and lack of supervision by ARP wardens. But what caused the panic? People were familiar with the sound of bombing, guns and the drone of aircraft. Why should 3 March have been any different? Despite the noise heard inside the shelter no German planes had been seen that night and there was no evidence of any bombs being dropped. Here was a community that had suffered for eighteen months the worst of the Blitz but as many people ran towards the shelter they recalled seeing a searchlight lighting up the sky and then hearing a huge explosion – such that they had never heard before. Many screamed and threw themselves to the ground.

What they actually heard was the salvo of rockets fired a quarter of a mile away at Victoria Park by an experimental new weapon. The local population had not been informed because of security regulations – a fact that some ex-veterans find hard to believe. Eyewitnesses described the sky being

The steps of Bethnal Green Station with the commemoration plaque above the entrance.

Bethnal Green Station memorial plaque.

lit up and the sound being terrifying. The Ministry of Defence confirmed that rockets were fired in Victoria Park but rejected the view that this caused the disaster. They claimed that the crush in the station was the result of sirens signalling a Luftwaffe attack. However, no one claimed they had heard any planes.

Coping with the crushed bodies was a truly dreadful and traumatic experience. Many babies and children that were brought out had turned blue. They were taken to the mortuary at Whitechapel on carts and buses. In nearly all cases death was due to asphyxiation with virtually all dying within ten to fifteen seconds of being crushed. Above the station is a small commemorative plaque, which was placed there in 1993 to the victims of the disaster although there is general feeling that it is inadequate and moves are afoot to erect a more befitting monument.

Years after the disaster there were reports of noises similar to those of women and children screaming. Our knowledge of strange incidents, whether they are related to Underground stations or buildings such as houses or churches, clearly depends on the extent to which they are reported or told to another party and we have to assume that many cases do not get reported. People tend to be reluctant in offering their stories for fear of what others might think or they try to rationalise their experience by looking for explanations such as the mind playing tricks or their imagination getting the better of them. In 1981 a station foreman was working late at Bethnal Green Station. He had seen to the usual tasks of securing the station and doing the paperwork when he heard the low sound of voices. As he stopped what he was doing the sound became more and more distinctive. It was the noise of children crying but it gradually grew louder and was then joined by the sound of women screaming. This went on for some ten to fifteen minutes until, overcome with fear, he left his office.

The sounds might be explained by the cacophony of noises often produced by the Underground such as the wind, motors or, if one is nearer the surface, the voices of people outside which can

The former site of the British Museum Station, now the Nationwide Building Society, High Holborn.

create distortion. However, to hear the sounds for over ten minutes and be able to describe them as the screams of women and children does raise doubts about these rational explanations, especially when the man, who had worked for many years on the Underground, was more than familiar with the sounds of the station.

BRITISH MUSEUM

A station with such an evocative name as 'British Museum' just had to be haunted especially by an Egyptian looking for a mummy. The station was located on Bury Place near to the museum and was opened in July 1900 by the Central London Railway and serviced what came to be known as the Central Line. With the opening of Holborn Station by the Great Northern, Piccadilly and Brompton Railway in 1906 less than 100yds away, and then the amalgamation of the lines under single management in 1933, it was decided to combine the stations. During the Second World War the platforms were bricked up to protect those sheltering from passing trains, though it would appear these walls were later removed. British Museum Station was used as a military administrative office and emergency command post up to the 1960s but it is now a disused station and cannot be accessed from the surface. In 1989 redevelopment of the area saw the demolition of the station at street level.

Before the closure of British Museum a rumour was circulated that the ghost of an Ancient Egyptian haunted the station dressed in a loincloth and headdress. He would emerge late at night and walk along the disused platform wailing as he went. It was said he was in search of a mummy, possibly a lost princess. As the story grew it caught the attention of a national newspaper who tried to keep the speculation and the interest going by offering a cash reward for anyone who would dare spend a night in the station. No doubt most people thought the story was a bit of fun but no one came forward to take up the challenge. Nonetheless the story did not end there.

This ghost story was related to the curse of Amen-Ra's tomb. The story involved the eerie goings-on with a mummy and the museum some fifty years earlier. The British Museum, which was established in 1753, houses the world's largest collection of Egyptian antiquities outside the Egyptian Museum in Cairo. They have formed part of the museum's collection since its foundation. Further antiquities from excavations came to the museum in the late nineteenth century and by 1924 the collection stood at 57,000 objects (that figure has since doubled). The story revolves around an exhibit still in the museum, a sarcophagus, or more appropriately the lid, the curse of the Egyptian Princess of Amen-Ra and for the stuff of a very imaginative conspiracy theory, the sinking of the *Titanic*. The story has been told with many variations as well as denials.

The coffin of the Egyptian Princess, who died in 1,050 BC, arrived at the British Museum in 1889. The label reads 'Painted wooden mummy-board of an unidentified woman.' As the *Titanic* crossed the Atlantic in April 1912 the English journalist William T. Stead (well known for exposing child abuse in the 1880s in the *Pall Mall Gazette*) told a ghost story about an Egyptian mummy and the translation of an inscription on the mummy's case. The inscription warned that anyone reciting it would meet a violent death. Worse still the mummy was on the *Titanic*! The story went that seven of the eight men who heard the story and Stead himself went down with the ship. The mummy in question was the remains of the Princess Amen-Ra, known as the 'Unlucky Mummy' because of the disasters associated with it. Amen-Ra, so the story goes, was donated to the British Museum (the British Museum claim that they only ever had the coffin lid, not the mummy). The arrival started a series of accidents involving workmen unloading the coffin – one broke his leg and another died shortly after despite his good health. Even when the princess was installed the trouble continued with reports by watchmen hearing the sounds of knocking and sobbing coming from the coffin. Watchmen began to leave their jobs and one died on duty. Soon the papers were on to the story. One photographer took a picture of the mummy case and when the photograph was developed the painting on the coffin was of a horrifying, human face.

Eventually the mummy was sold to an American archaeologist who arranged for its removal to New York. In April 1912, the new owner escorted its treasure aboard the *Titanic*. The story has been embellished in its telling but was it really nothing more than an elaborate ghost story created by Stead and his friend Douglas Murray? They sold the story to the press who were not particularly bothered about whether it was true or not – it was a good tale and they published it. The *Washington Post* (17 August 1980) even made reference to it years later when attempts were being made to salvage remains of the *Titanic* which were thwarted by storms and bad weather: 'Some hunters have spoken darkly of the famous mummy that was allegedly on board, saying it transferred the curse of all who disturbed its grave to the vessel's maiden voyage and to all search efforts,' reported the *Post*.

The so called 'curse of Tutankhamen' had for many years provided the press with stories of untimely deaths after the discovery of the tomb by Howard Carter in 1922. Films at the time such as *The Mummy* (1932) and *The Mummy's Tomb* (1942) all added to the fascination. The British Museum Underground Station ghost in search of a mummy proved to be an irresistible story not only for the press but also for film and literature. Writing in *British Horror Cinema* (2001 ed. S. Chibnall), Marcelle Perks comments that the film *Bulldog Jack* spoofed 1933 press reports that the British Museum Station was haunted by an Egyptian ghost (some discrepancy in dating here as *Bulldog Jack* was not released until 1935).

The film was a comedy thriller starring Ralph Richardson, Fay Wray and Jack Hulbert. The plot revolves around Bulldog Drummond who is injured when his sabotaged car crashes and Jack Pennington (Jack Hulbert) agrees to masquerade as Drummond. He is enlisted to help Ann Manders (Fay Wray) find her grandfather who has been kidnapped by a gang of crooks who want him to copy a valuable necklace they plan to steal. The plan goes wrong in the British Museum and the film climaxes in an exciting chase on a runaway train in the London Underground, which also features a secret passage leading into a sarcophagus in the museum. The story of the Egyptian ghost in the

Above: The British Museum, established in 1753 and opened to the public in 1759.

Left: W.T. Stead (1849-1912). Did he concoct the ghost story about the curse of Princess Amen-Ra?

station also features in the novel by Keith Lowe, *Tunnel Vision* (Arrow Books, 2001), when the lead character, who has to travel to every tube station on the system in a single day after a drunken bet, tells his girlfriend that the sound of Egyptian voices can be heard floating down the tunnel.

Some accounts rate the British Museum ghost as the scariest of all the ghost stories on the Underground. We disagree. The essence of a ghost story or experience is a combination of it being believable and yet also understated. The idea of an Egyptian ghost dressed in loincloth and headdress looking for a (dubious) mummy on the platform of a station does not meet these requirements. It's not a bad tale and, like the curse of Amen-Ra, it is testimony to the power of the press to generate a good, but fictitious story – something the press has been very adept at doing for years.

COVENT GARDEN

The very busy Covent Garden Underground Station was opened on 11 April 1907, four months after the start of the Great Northern, Piccadilly & Brompton Railway services in December 1906. The station, which is now on the Piccadilly Line, was designed by architect Leslie Green and is easily recognisable by the distinctive red-glazed façade. The station is between Holborn and Leicester Square (the journey between Covent Garden and Leicester Square is the shortest distance between two adjacent stations on the Underground). The platforms are accessed primarily by lift (an important point later in relation to a particular ghostly experience) and moves are afoot (2008) to redevelop parts of the station to cope with the heavy use of commuters and tourists.

Although the modern-day Covent Garden has its roots in the seventeenth century, the area that tourists visit today was renovated from the 1970s. Nonetheless the square, with St Paul's Church to the west, is still recognisable in eighteenth-century drawings. Designed by the great architect Inigo Jones (1573-1652), Covent Garden came to be dominated by the market with the present-day Piazza built in 1830. On 12 April 1665 the first victim of the Great Plague, Margaret Porteous, was buried in St Paul's Church. Covent Garden was a centre of small businesses and in particular coach makers. Not surprisingly the Underground station was built on what was once a coach maker's workshop.

A ghost that floats above ground in Covent Garden is that of a nun. Actor Bob Hoskins, who used to work as a porter in Covent Garden, recalled how, in the late 1950s, he encountered the ghost. He was working in a cellar when he saw a woman's face appear on the wall. Wearing a nun's habit she reached out to him with upturned hands and spoke, although he could not recall what she said. He told the *Guardian* (9 October 1999) in an interview that he learned that the area used to be called Convent Garden because the Benedictines of Westminster owned it. He added that, according to local superstition, anyone seeing the nun would have a charmed life. It seemed to work for Bob.

For some Victorian commentators the Underground would bring us closer to the Devil in the disruption of not only burial grounds but also by what was seen as the descent into Hades. Covent Garden had a very popular and influential minister in Revd Dr John Cumming (1807-1881). Between 1832 and 1879 he was minister of the National Scottish Church and spent much of his time in preaching prophecies about the end of the world. 'Why not build an overhead Railway? ... It's better to wait for the Devil than to make roads down into Hell', he stormed. In another of his writings in 1860 he commented that, '... the forthcoming end of the world will be hastened by the construction of underground railways burrowing into infernal regions and thereby disturbing the Devil'.

Covent Garden Station, the haunt of nineteenth-century actor William Terriss.

St Paul's Church ('The Actors' Church'), Covent Garden, built by Inigo Jones, has been there since 1633. The first-known victim of the plague of 1665–1666, Margaret Ponteous, was buried in the churchyard in April 1665.

Covent Garden. The main building in the Piazza was erected in 1830 although the glass roof did not come until the 1870s.

Covent Garden has a long association with the theatre. The oldest established is the Theatre Royal, Drury Lane, which had its origins in a patent granted on the Restoration of the Monarchy in 1660. Other theatres followed and it was this association that provided one of the most famous ghosts of the Underground, that of actor William Terriss (1847-1897).

William Terriss, whose real name was William Charles James Lewin, was a popular leading actor of melodramas as well as being a dapper and fashionable man often known by his trademark white gloves and cape. Described as having a 'handsome presence, fine voice and gallant bearing', he was eminently suited for the stage. Terriss had a regular routine that he followed each day and this would include visiting a bakery which used to stand on the site of the station – a place he kept coming back to after his death (the station was not built until eight years after his murder). Despite him being the darling of audiences he clearly had enemies who envied his success. One particular enemy was Richard Archer Prince.

Richard Prince was a struggling actor who had become increasingly mentally unstable and had acquired the nickname 'Mad Archer'. Such was the state of Prince's desperation that by December 1897 he had pawned his clothes, save for what he wore. Prince received a letter from the Actors' Benevolent Fund (ABF) on 16 December stating that they were ending his grant. The ABF recorded what happened when Prince turned up at their office in Adam Street demanding money on the day of the murder. The secretary had refused Prince any money when he then 'simply crossed over

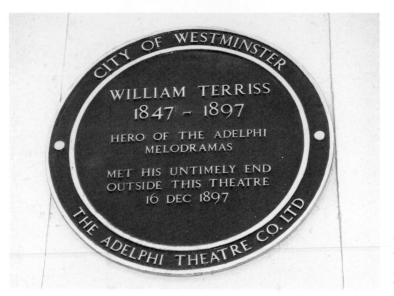

The plaque to William Terriss near the stage door of the Adelphi Theatre.

the Strand to Maiden Lane where he knew Terriss had his own private entrance to the Adelphi Theatre separate from the Stage Door in Bull Inn Court, and waited for him to turn up for the evening performance.' As the unknowing Terriss entered his private door, 'Prince ran up to him and stabbed him three times with a knife.' A crowd quickly pounced on Prince whilst a doctor attended to Terriss but it was in vain and he died a few minutes later, a life cut short by murder. Prince told the arresting policeman, 'He has had due warning, and if he is dead, he knew what to expect from me. He prevented me getting money from the Fund today, and I have stopped him.' A plaque on the wall commemorates Terriss by the stage door of the Adelphi Theatre which records the event of the murder.

At the Old Bailey on 13 January 1898 Prince was advised to plead not guilty. His defence as well as various witnesses, including his mother, attempted to prove insanity. The jury declared him to be guilty but not responsible for his actions and he was sent to Broadmoor where he managed to become involved in entertaining the inmates as well as conducting the prison orchestra.

The ghost of Terriss began to haunt both the Adelphi Theatre and Covent Garden Station. Strange noises, lights going on and off, the sound of footsteps as well as sightings of Terriss have been experienced at the theatre. Many staff at the station have reported incidents after it has been closed to passengers at night with the ghost manifesting itself in a number of ways. The sound of disembodied gasps and sighs, knocking in the lift and sightings of a ghost-like image of a man were some of the manifestations.

Peter Underwood, probably Britain's leading authority and writer on the paranormal, records in his book, *Haunted London* (1975), an account told to him by an Underground ticket collector, Jack Hayden. On a cold November night in 1955 after the last train had gone, Jack was locking the gates when he suddenly saw a tall, distinguished man with a very sad face and sunken cheeks ascending the emergency stairs towards him. When Jack realised the man might be locked in, he shouted to him and told the man to wait and he would let him out. However, by the time Jack undid the gate the man was nowhere to be seen. Four days later Jack saw the man again wearing an old-fashioned

Above: The Adelphi Theatre stage door near to where Terriss was murdered by Richard Prince.

Right: The Adelphi Theatre which is also reputed to be haunted by the ghost of William Terriss.

grey suit and some light-coloured gloves. Jack asked the figure if he needed the cloakroom but he did not answer and just moved away and disappeared within seconds. Understandably Jack was reluctant to tell anyone of his experience for fear of ridicule. It was only another few days after the second sighting that Jack and one of the guards heard a screaming noise. It came from a nineteen-year-old Underground worker, Victor Locker. Victor came into the mess room looking as though he had seen a ghost – which he had. He described it as a tall, strange-looking man. At this point Jack made a report and the management sent a foreman, Eric Davey, to check what had happened. Eric, by coincidence, was an amateur spiritualist who saw the ghost himself some days later. Eric and Jack described the ghost to an artist who drew an image of the man which was then passed on to *Psychic News*. They in turn looked through photographs which they showed to Eric and Jack. Both recognised the man they saw in the Underground. It was William Terriss.

It was reported in the *Sunday Dispatch* in January 1956 that the ghost of a tall man wearing white gloves was seen in Covent Garden London Underground Station. It added that member of staff 'Victor Locker, a West African, who believes he saw a ghost, cannot bear to work at the station. His application for a transfer to another station was granted immediately.' Victor described the experience like that of heavy weight pressing down on him leaving him helpless. In the Channel Five documentary, *Ghosts of the Underground* (2006), another ex-Underground worker, a lift operator, described a very similar experience to the others. He too saw a tall man in old-fashioned clothes in 1972 and, like Jack Hayden, when he was shown a photograph of William Terriss he instantly recognised it as the man he saw.

There have been no reported sightings of the ghost of William Terriss since. We can only speculate as to why this might be but it does coincide with a time when Covent Garden went through a period of crisis. From the 1960s traffic congestion had become a huge problem, particularly for lorries delivering and distributing goods at the large fruit and vegetable market. The area was threatened with major redevelopment but a public outcry pressured the Home Secretary, Robert Carr, in 1973 to give Listed Building status to many places around the square thus preventing the proposed redevelopment. Maybe William's ghost came to rest but we should not get too complacent, as changes to develop the station are due to take place and may provoke the ghost of Terriss into a new burst of activity.

ELEPHANT AND CASTLE

The Elephant and Castle Underground Station is located in the Borough of Southwark. It is on the Bank branch of the Northern Line and is also the southern terminus for the Bakerloo Line. The station was built in two stages. The Northern Line (then the City & South London Railway) was opened in December 1890 and the Bakerloo Line (Baker Street and Waterloo Railway) opened in August 1906. The Elephant and Castle Station is a typical Leslie Green structure which remains much as when it was originally constructed.

The ghost associated with the station probably lacks the eeriness of some of the other haunted stations. It is not a known individual who died at or near the station as, for example, the Covent Garden or Aldgate ghosts. Staff who work at the station have experienced the sounds of someone running towards them mainly when the station is closed but no one can be seen. In addition there are other unexplained noises including doors suddenly opening.

Right: Elephant and Castle Station where the ghostly sounds of someone running have been heard, as well as the appearance of a young woman boarding a train but then disappearing.

Below: An empty corridor at the Elephant and Castle Station.

A lone young female has been seen by commuters and staff late at night entering the carriage of a train but is never seen leaving – as if she disappears. One tube worker recorded his experience. He joined the train at the Elephant and Castle to travel with the driver. As the driver had not arrived the man then went to the rear door to wait for him. It was then that he saw a girl getting into the carriage and walking by him. Soon after the driver turned up and the two men walked to the front of the train. The man then noted that the girl was not in the carriage, 'she could not have left the train without passing me – I had full view of the carriage and platform at the time.' The only place she could have gone, he said, was down the tunnel. Growing more agitated he told the driver about the girl who responded with, 'Oh, her. We hear about her all the time.'

One worker who had previously worked at Blackfriars was so scared by his experiences at the station he refused to do night duty there. Another night-duty worker reported hearing the sound of footsteps getting louder and then becoming fainter as they ran off into the distance of the platform. He added that this occurred especially on winter evenings.

A chilling site for anyone travelling alone is to look at a carriage window and be confronted with the sudden reflection of a ghost-life face staring back even though no one is sitting nearby. People travelling northbound on the Bakerloo Line from the Elephant and Castle have reported this particular apparition on many occasions.

FARRINGDON

The ghost of Anne Naylor haunts Farringdon Station. This station is on the Metropolitan, Hammersmith & City and Circle Lines between King's Cross and Barbican. It was opened in January 1863 as the terminus for the original Metropolitan Railway – the world's first underground railway. Initially called Farringdon Street it was relocated in December 1865 when the Metropolitan Railway opened an extension to Moorgate. Renamed Farringdon and High Holborn in January 1922 (this name is still on the façade) it changed to its present name in April 1936.

It is located near Smithfield Market, which itself has a rich and interesting history. Smithfield from the fourteenth century had been home to tournaments and duels as well as the debauchery and rowdiness associated with the famous Bartholomew Fair (1133-1855) held in mid- to late August. Smithfield was, for over 400 years, one of the main sites of executions, including that of William Wallace ('Braveheart') in 1305. It is also the site of a plague pit.

The story of thirteen-year-old Anne Naylor (spelt Ann Nailor at the trial at the Old Bailey) is one of dreadful cruelty. Anne was apprenticed as milliner to Sarah Metyard and her daughter, Sarah Morgan Metyard. In 1758 there were five young girls in her employment all of whom had come from parish workhouses including Anne and her sister. Anne was described as being of a sickly disposition and therefore found the work difficult and could not keep up with the other girls. This singled her out and made her become the object of the fury of the evil Sarah Metyard and daughter. They punished Anne with such barbarity and repeated acts of cruelty that she decided to leave. Unfortunately she did not get far and was brought back where she was confined in an upstairs room and fed with little more than bread and water. For such a sickly child this could only weaken her further. Again Anne seized a chance to escape. Once in the street she ran to a milk carrier and begged him to protect her, telling him of her cruel employers who would starve and beat her if she was returned.

Farringdon Station where the screams of poor Anne Naylor have been heard.

Anne had chosen the wrong person to plead to for help and he handed her back. Poor Anne could only imagine the horrors that awaited her. Thrown back into her room she awaited the fury of the Metyards. As the old women held her down the daughter began to beat Anne savagely with a broom handle. They then tied her hands behind her and fastened her to door and left her there for three days without food or water. Threatened with punishment the other apprentices were not allowed to go anywhere near the room. Alone, bruised, exhausted and starved, by the fourth day she died.

Despite the warnings, some of the other girls saw her body tied with cord and hanging from the door. They cried out to the sadistic women to help Anne. The daughter ran upstairs and proceeded to hit the dead Anne with a shoe. It was apparent that there was no sign of life and pathetic attempts were made at reviving her. One of the young apprentices, Philadelphia Dowley, acted as a witness four years later (July 1762) at the trial of Anne's murder at the Old Bailey. When asked why Anne tried to run away she replied, 'because she was ... so ill. She used to be beat with a walking stick and hearth brooms by the mother, and go without her victuals.' Another witness, Richard Rooker, had been a lodger at Metyard's house. He told of the grisly attempt to conceal the crime, the revelation of other murders and how Metyard's daughter had told him with great reluctance what happened:

> She told me that these children were starved to death; that Ann Nailor died first, whom the mother would not bury; and the reason the mother gave for it, she said, was, because it would be clear evidence that she was starved to death, by the appearance of the body ... a few hours after the body

Smithfield Market near Farringdon Station has been the site of a meat market for over 800 years. The area also held public executions, had a plague pit and was the site of the famous Bartholomew Fair.

was carried up stairs into the garret, and locked up in a box, where it was kept for upwards of two months, till it putrefied, and maggots came from her.

He went on to describe how he was told that the mother removed the body and tried to cut it to pieces and then burned one of the hands in the fire. Then 'she tied the body and head in a brown cloth, and the other parts in another, being part of the bed furniture [and] carried them to Chick Lane gully-hole'.(Chick Lane was removed in the mid-nineteenth century and absorbed into what is now Charterhouse Street – close to Farringdon Station). Unable to get rid of the body parts she left them in the mud collected in the grate of a sewer. It was the remains of this evidence that were discovered by a nightwatchman who reported it to the 'constable of the night' – Thomas Lovegrove, overseer of the parish of St Andrew, Holborn. The coroner assumed the body parts to be those of a corpse stolen from a churchyard.

Four years elapsed after Anne's murder and it seemed that she would be denied justice for her brutal murder. It may well have stayed that way had it not being for the continual disagreements between the mother and daughter. The arguments resulted in frequent beatings for the young Sarah Metyard, who was so provoked that she wrote a letter to the overseers of Tottenham Parish informing them about the whole affair and that her mother was a murderer. Both mother and daughter were subsequently arrested. In the trial the Metyards were also indicted for the wilful murder of Mary Nailor, Anne's sister, aged eight years old.

In her defence the mother admitted that Anne was ill and that she and her daughter took Anne 'and laid her on the bed … She had victuals carried her up every day … She never died in my house.' Her daughter claimed differently. 'I begged of my mother to let her have some supper … She said she should have none … I believed the girl would die, for she went up stairs upon all fours, she was so weak.' The year in which the Metyard's were arrested (1762) also witnessed the so-called sensation of the Cock Lane Ghost in Smithfield. This story, later revealed as a fraud, captured the imagination of many. In court a witness told of how he had heard the young Metyard say some odd things about the Cock Lane story, 'Mother, you are the Chick Lane ghost; remember the gully-hole' – a reference to the place nearby where Anne's body had been dumped.

Mother and daughter were sentenced to be executed at Tyburn (near to where Marble Arch now stands) and then taken to the Surgeon's Hall for dissection. The daughter 'pleaded her belly' [pregnancy] but after an inspection by matrons they confirmed she was not with child. On Monday 19 July they were led from Newgate Prison in a cart on the two-mile journey to Tyburn. The mother was described as being in a fit during the journey and 'left this life in a state of insensibility.' As for her daughter she wept incessantly from leaving Newgate until the moment of her death on the scaffold. After the execution both were 'conveyed in a hearse to Surgeons' Hall, where they were exposed to the curiosity of the public, and then dissected.'

The deprivations and eventual horrors that poor Anne endured in her brief life are heartbreaking. Brought up in a parish workhouse with her young sister then apprenticed to the horrendous Sarah Metyard only to be beaten, imprisoned, starved and left to die, her brief life was harsh and short of any human compassion. In death she was subjected to the butchery of her sadistic employer. One would like to believe that she found peace but it appears her tormented soul wanders Farringdon Station where she has been nicknamed the 'Screaming Spectre'. Over the years, there have been regular reports of the ghost of Anne, the sound of her screams echoing down the platform and passengers claiming to hear the screaming of a young girl as the last train leaves the station at night.

HIGHGATE

Highgate Underground Station is situated on Archway Road. Since this is the southern end of the A1 or Great North Road, the area resounds day and night to the permanent uproar and nightmarish bedlam that this road creates. The station is not particularly convenient for the centre of Highgate Village. The village is famous, among other things, for the ghost of the featherless chicken which, for centuries, has inhabited Pond Square, occasionally pecking anyone who happens to be about at the time.

The world-famous Highgate Cemetery has ghosts galore. Its sleeping inmates include the scientist Michael Faraday (1791-1867), Mary Ann Evans (1819-1880), the novelist with a controversial lifestyle who operated under the pseudonym 'George Eliot', and the eminent actors Sir Ralph Richardson (1902-1983) and Sir Michael Redgrave (1908-1985). Perhaps the best-known occupant of the cemetery is Karl Marx (1818-1883), the great German social, economic and political theorist. It is to be hoped that they all rest in peace.

Highgate stands in the Northern Heights to the north-east of Hampstead Heath and the top of Highgate Hill is over 400ft above sea level. The village has long been a highly desirable and therefore very expensive residential quarter and a number of fine houses of the sixteenth to the twentieth centuries survive.

The infamous Tyburn Tree where thousands of people met their end.

Near the site of the infamous Tyburn Gallows, close to Marble Arch. It was here that Sarah Metyard and her daughter were executed in 1762 for the murder of Anna Naylor.

Platform, Farringdon Station.

Entrance to the Egyptian Avenue at Highgate Cemetery. The famous cemetery has many ghosts.

The railway history of Highgate is a little complicated. The first station bearing 'Highgate' as its name opened in June 1907 and it was the terminus of a branch of the Charing Cross, Euston and Hampstead Railway from Camden Town. This station is the present Archway of the Northern Line. The line was extended beyond Archway to East Finchley in 1939 and to High Barnet in 1940, but not before Archway had enjoyed short spells being officially but confusingly known as Highgate (Archway) and then Archway (Highgate).

However, Archway Station is some distance from the present Highgate Northern Line Station, being at the bottom of the hill on which the village of Highgate stands. Highgate tube station did not open when the Northern was extended in 1939 but instead began operations on 19 June 1941. The Highgate railway ghosts, however, have not been reported from this particular Northern Line station but another station very close by and actually above it!

The key to this seemingly confused situation lies in the presence nearby of the Alexandra Palace. After the Great Exhibition which was held in Hyde Park in 1851, the building in which it was housed, universally known as the 'Crystal Palace', was taken down and a few years later re-erected in enlarged form on Sydenham Hill in South London. The palace and its grounds quickly became a major attraction especially at weekends and bank holidays.

Naturally, anything that the South Londoners could do the North Londoners thought they could do better and the decision was taken to build a rival on and around a hill, over 300ft in height, between Hornsey and New Southgate. The building opened in 1873 and within days was largely destroyed by fire. This somehow typified the 'Ally Pally's' luck. It went on to undergo some ups and a lot of downs with which we need not concern ourselves. The relevant point is that it was thought likely to attract a lot of visitors and also new local residents as the area opened up for middle-class housing development. It is therefore not surprising that a number of proposals were made for railway lines that would approach Alexandra Palace from the south. Putting it in simple terms, two nominally independent companies built a line from Finsbury Park via Crouch End, Highgate and Muswell Hill to Alexandra Palace. The line to Highgate opened in 1867 and to Alexandra Palace in 1873. Both were operated from the start by the Great Northern Railway.

Rather like the 'Ally Pally', the branch line had mixed fortunes and neither the Great Northern nor its successor, the London & North Eastern Railway, quite seemed to know what to do with it. Consequently the LNER was probably relieved when in 1935 a long-standing idea turned into a concrete proposal. First of all this involved the transfer of the LNER lines to High Barnet and Edgware to the jurisdiction of London Transport who would electrify them as an extension of the Northern Line tube from Archway. The extension between Archway and East Finchley opened early in July 1939 but the new station at Highgate was not ready for public use until 1941. Even then it was incomplete.

The Alexandra Palace branch was added to this scheme at a later date. A considerable amount of preliminary work was done but in the austere economic conditions that prevailed after the Second World War, the modernisation of the branch somehow slipped through the net. The decision not to proceed with electrification was taken in 1953 and the LNER and then the Eastern Region of British Railways continued to operate rather antiquated steam trains to Alexandra Palace until the passenger service was withdrawn in 1954. The puff, however, had most certainly gone out of them by that time. Freight services were withdrawn some years later. Had the Alexandra Palace branch been electrified, it is likely that it would still be a useful part of the Underground network.

The Highgate Northern Line Station was somewhat lower than the high-level Alexandra Palace branch platforms at Highgate and escalators joined the tube platforms with those used by the

Boarded-up tunnel mouth at the north end of abandoned Highgate Station. The line from here to Alexandra Palace was due to become part of the Northern Line, but in the event this never happened.

LNER/British Railways trains. The intention was that another escalator would reach to street level but this had to wait until 1957.

As part of the preliminary electrification and modernisation work for the Alexandra Palace branch, the Highgate LNER station was rebuilt in a modern concrete idiom. Conductor rails were in position for much of the route from Highgate towards Alexandra Palace, as were supports for lineside cables, but the power was never switched on. Highgate LNER station stood in a cutting with tunnels at either ends of the platforms and even after its total rebuilding it always seemed to be a bit dark, damp and unwelcoming. This part of London is hilly and possesses many large, mature trees which help to add areas of shade and a considerable sense of atmosphere.

It is this station which seems to be haunted; voices have been heard; people down there have related how they felt they were being watched by invisible but malevolent eyes. There have also been occasional reports of the sound of passing steam trains long after the track was lifted. Those claiming to have heard such noises were often people living in houses backing onto the line. The sounds of voices have been heard on many occasions not only at Highgate but also where the intermediate stations had once been situated. This was particularly understandable where noises were heard in the neighbourhood of Muswell Hill. The locals there were among the most vehement protestors when plans were publicised to close the line although the truth was that they did not actually use the services very much.

The track formation between the intermediate stations at Cranley Gardens and Muswell Hill is in use as a public footpath.

HYDE PARK CORNER

The Great Northern, Piccadilly and Brompton Railway opened on 15 December 1906. It was created out of an amalgamation of the Brompton & Piccadilly Circus and the Great Northern and Strand Railways. A new piece of line was inserted between Piccadilly Circus and the vicinity of Holborn to give through running at that time between Finsbury Park and Hammersmith. This route formed the nucleus of the later much-extended Piccadilly Line.

Early one morning in the 1970s a couple of maintenance workers on the night shift at Hyde Park Corner tube station were enjoying a well-earned rest with a mug of tea in the staff office. At that time the station entrance was locked to prevent public entry and all was quiet when they were amazed to hear the sound of the escalator in motion. They had just spent a couple of hours doing repair work on it. This had necessitated switching the power off and yet here was the selfsame escalator moving, something which clearly it could only do if the power had been restored. No one else was on the premises. How did this happen?

Although this particular occurrence seems to have been a one-off, staff who work at this station report there are one or two strange spots which are inexplicably cold, even on the hottest of summer days. Staff manning the station when it opens early in the morning or towards the end of services at night, claim that they have sensed what they describe as 'evil forces' and that they are being observed by unseen eyes. Some workers have also reported a part of the station where the sound of girls crying can sometimes be heard, often when the station is closed to passengers at night. They try to avoid that part of the station at these times.

Hyde Park Corner tube is very handy for those who like a ghost with their pint of beer. Tucked away off the beaten track but close to the station is The Grenadier pub in Wilton Row. Although

The rebuilt high-level Underground platforms at Highgate that never saw underground trains. It would not be easy to get a better view as they don't want you to see it.

Footpath along the track bed of the abandoned 'Ally Pally' branch near Cranley Gardens. Ghostly steam trains have been heard on windy nights.

Former entrance of Hyde Park Corner on Knightsbridge, now used as a restaurant.

there are dozens of London pubs with stories of hauntings, that of The Grenadier is among the best known. The pub was once the officers' mess for the nearby barracks of the Duke of Wellington's Regiment. On one occasion, an officer was caught cheating at cards. In their rather curious code of honour and conduct, the officers regarded such behaviour as that of an out-and-out bounder and cad. Those present decided to mete out rough justice there and then. He was flogged, beaten up and ejected from the front door, only to die shortly afterwards of his injuries. His ghost moved in and stayed when the barracks was converted to a pub. September, which was the month of his death, is the best time for those keen to make his acquaintance. Not only have successive landlords reported the build-up of an 'atmosphere' and inexplicable bangs and knocks as August turns into September but a shadowy black figure has manifested itself on many occasions, even terrifying the formidable German shepherd dog which one landlord kept as a guard against intruders. On one occasion, no less a dignitary than a chief superintendent of Scotland Yard was prepared to go on record as having said that he had witnessed the ghost. Such a public utterance might be viewed by the top brass of the constabulary with some disapproval. Perhaps the officer knew by this time that his career was going no further and that he had nothing to lose.

ICKENHAM

Ickenham is a bijou outer suburb which manages to retain some semblance of its previously rural village character. Running through the parish is the little river Pinn. The present parish church dates from the fourteenth century and remains small, an indication that Ickenham was a tiny settlement until the Metropolitan Railway came along and started the process whereby it would change forever. Large-scale residential development began in the 1920s with the sale of a number of sizeable country estates. Nearby is Swakeleys, a great Jacobean mansion completed in 1638 and now offices.

With services on both the Metropolitan and Piccadilly Lines, Ickenham lies not far from the western extremity of these lines, being the last but one stop before Uxbridge. The Metropolitan Line station opened on 25 September 1905. At first, befitting the essentially rustic nature of the place, no station had been provided and when, responding somewhat reluctantly to local protests, a stopping place was opened by the company, it was designated a mere 'halt'. Few people used it and the Metropolitan Railway erected a flagpole complete with a large red flag to let potential passengers know that trains halted there. On one occasion, the flag flapped so wildly in the wind that a horse being led along a nearby road bolted, injuring the man leading it. After a civil action, the Metropolitan was ordered to take the flag down. Piccadilly Line services began running on 23 October 1933.

On the face of it, Ickenham and its modest station, rebuilt in the early 1970s, seem reassuringly ordinary, perhaps even sedate, most definitely not the locale for a haunting. Impressions can be deceptive. One morning in 1951 during the night-time hours when the station was closed to passengers, an electrician was busily engaged in maintenance work on the platform. His was lonely work and even a man with little imagination might occasionally have wondered if there was anything lurking menacingly beyond the comforting pool of light shed by the lamp close by. He worked away stolidly, accustomed to what would now be called 'antisocial hours' and the blanket of silence and the sense of emptiness which descended on the Underground in the hiatus between the last trains of the previous day and the first of the morrow.

He may have been of a stoical nature but even he was rather startled when, standing up for a moment and looking round, he saw a middle-aged woman close by and apparently watching him with considerable interest. He thought that her clothes were a trifle old-fashioned and there was enough light for him to note that she wore a red scarf. The woman, apparently aware that he had noticed her, then gestured for him to follow her. Perhaps thinking that she was a benighted traveller who had arrived on the last train and had somehow contrived to be locked in when the station closed down for the night, the electrician followed her along the platform, keen to help. Not a word was said as he followed her up the stairs but no sooner had she reached the last step than she vanished into thin air. The electrician, bewildered and not a little frightened, was left wondering what he had seen or even whether he had actually seen anything at all.

It was little solace to him to learn that the woman with the red scarf had been glimpsed many times over the years by other London transport workers. They thought that she was the ghost of a woman who, many years earlier, had fallen from the platform and died instantly when she hit the electrified rail. Belated passengers arriving at Ickenham on the last trains of the night also claim to have caught sight of the figure of a woman, some distance away, gesticulating to get their attention but once she had got it, vanishing.

Ickenham looking towards Uxbridge. An unlikely location for a haunting?

KENNINGTON

Kennington is a mixed, largely residential district of south London with a history dating back to Norman times. Today's visitor could be forgiven for thinking that there was nothing there before the nineteenth century. In fact Kennington Common was the location for many public hangings. These attracted large crowds and the present St Mark's Church stands on the site of the gallows. Kennington Park stands on part of the old common.

Kennington was an intermediate station on the City & South London Railway which opened in 1890. This line was the world's first electric tube railway and, with some minor changes, it went on to become the Bank branch of the Northern Line. In 1926 a new piece of the tube network arrived at Kennington. This was in the form of an extension under the Thames and via Waterloo of the old Charing Cross, Euston and Hampstead Railway. Both routes became part of the Northern Line in 1937.

A feature of Kennington which is little known to the travelling public is the Kennington Loop. This was built as part of the extension from Charing Cross and is a complicated, or some would say delightfully simple, means of ensuring that the paths of trains on both the southbound routes of the Northern Line do not conflict where they come together at Kennington. Southbound trains from the Charing Cross direction travel in a tunnel under the tube tunnels containing the City Branch lines and then run into their own platform at Kennington. They can then continue southwards by joining the line in the Morden direction but many of them terminate at Kennington. After ensuring

Above left: The original street-level building at Kennington built by the City & South London Railway. It is the only station on this line to have kept its distinctive dome feature.

Above right: Empty Northern Line train entering Kennington loop.

that all passengers have been detrained, the drivers of the terminating trains then advance into the single-line tunnel which plunges under the Morden route and then literally loops back on itself so that northbound Charing Cross trains are now facing in the right direction without having caused any conflicting traffic movements.

Trains for the Charing Cross route have their own platform at Kennington. However, it is sometimes necessary to keep the empty trains at signals before admitting them to this northbound platform. Train crew do not like the loop. Its sharp curves mean that the wheels emit a loud and irksome flange squeal accentuated by the narrow confines of the tube. More sinister, however, are the frequent reports from train crews about the threatening atmosphere in the loop. Passengers are never allowed to travel round the loop but despite that, the men and women working trains along this piece of line are sometimes seriously disconcerted by not always being sure they are alone. The worst place for mysterious sounds and an evil atmosphere is when the empty trains are standing at the signal awaiting clearance to enter the Charing Cross platform. Tube trains are of course now one-person operated but a number of drivers who have followed procedure, and ensured that all passengers have alighted at the southbound-side platform, have heard the sound of doors between the carriages being opened and closed while their trains were waiting at the signals to enter the Charing Cross platform. Who or what opened and closed these doors?

King William Street facing Monument Station. The vast underground tunnel that links Bank Station and
Monument Station runs the length of King William Street. Are there, as some people have commented,
distinct spectral figures seen among the shadows?

A crowd flowed over London Bridge, so many,
I had not thought death had undone so many.
Sighs, short and infrequent, were exhaled,
And each man fixed his eyes before his feet.
Flowed up the hill and down King William Street …

T.S. Eliot, *The Waste Land* (1922)

KING WILLIAM STREET

King William Street, EC4, was laid out between 1829 and 1835 to provide an approach to then new
London Bridge and it was named after the monarch of the time, the rather vacuous William IV who
reigned from 1830-1837.

The tube station that formerly stood in this street was the City terminus of the City & South
London Railway which ran under the Thames to Stockwell on the Surrey Shore, a distance of
around three-and-a-half miles. This line was of international historical importance as the world's
first successful underground electric railway. It opened in 1890 but closed in 1900 when the line was
extended in a northerly direction to Moorgate on a different alignment. It was thus an extremely

early railway closure so it has had more time than most to gather its ghosts. The station stood at the junction of King William Street and what is now Monument Street. The building that housed the station facilities at street level has long since gone.

King William Street was a quaint little station with its wooden platforms, bijou locomotives and uninviting carriages known as 'padded cells' and it provided a host of operating problems, but even after trains were withdrawn it found ways to continue serving Londoners, even if it did so in a quiet, understated way. Commenting on the waste involved in such an early closure, *The Railway Magazine* of February 1901 asked whether or not the station and its associated tunnels could be used for the growing of mushrooms or as secure bonded warehouses. It slumbered on, however, without finding any such users, but hit the headlines in 1914 when someone who probably should have known better, that is the editor of the self-same *Railway Magazine,* suggested that the station and its tunnels contained a cell of ruthless enemy agents who, armed to the teeth with weapons and explosives, were planning to launch their own campaign of ethnic cleansing on the good folk living and working in the City. This absurd claim was taken seriously by the police and a search was undertaken but nothing untoward was found.

The idea of these tunnels and platforms gathering dust and memories while existing in a state of suspended animation under the hustle and bustle of the City's streets excited considerable public interest. In 1930 a privileged group of journalists was given a guided tour and found that much of what was below ground was just as it would have been when the closure took place, except that it was dirtier and somewhat damper. Perhaps most eerie was the signal box. This had twenty-two manually operated levers and was virtually intact.

Parts of the station below ground and its associated running tunnels were extensively modified and acted as air-raid shelters during the Second World War. When hostilities ended, the owners of the new office block at street level where the station had been all those years ago found that the subterranean parts of the station provide ideal conditions for the safe storage of documents.

The tube tunnels running to King William Street slumber on, gathering stalactites as the years pass by. Access to what is left below ground is strictly limited but those who have managed to gain entry have spoken about indistinct spectral figures seen among the shadows. Psychic mediums in the 1970s and 1980s claim they have made contact with one or more ghosts. In the whole of greater London, there are surely few other locations more redolent of the supernatural than what is left of the subterranean parts of this pioneering tube station, so long closed to the public and so long the haunt of who knows what?

LIVERPOOL STREET

Liverpool Street, as well as being a large, impressive and busy mainline terminus, is an important nodal point on the Underground being served by the tube Central Line and the Metropolitan, Circle and Hammersmith and City sub-surface lines. The first Underground trains here began running in 1875. They were operated by the Metropolitan Railway and at first ran into the Great Eastern Railway's station. Soon afterwards they commenced running into the Metropolitan's own station, then called 'Bishopsgate'. In 1912 trains of the Central London Railway began to serve Liverpool Street.

Liverpool Street Station stands on the site of the Bethlehem Royal Hospital which was founded in 1247 as the Priory of St Mary Bethlehem. It seems that the infirmary attached to the priory

Liverpool Street Station entrance from Bishopgate.

first started treating mental patients around 1377 although the methods they employed for therapy would strike us today as nothing less than barbaric. In 1676 the hospital moved to a site close by at Moorfields and it was then known as 'Bedlam'. It made a lot of money from allowing paying visitors to watch the antics of the inmates and to egg them on to perform obscene and other repulsive acts, all of which the patrons found highly diverting. William Hogarth (1697-1764) immortalised Bedlam when, in 1732-33, he painted a scene based on it as the eighth illustration in his pictorial saga *The Rake's Progress.*

The station precincts are supposedly haunted by the screams of a woman said to have been incarcerated in Bedlam in the 1780s, although by this time the hospital had of course moved to Moorfields. However, an inconvenient little fact like that should never be allowed to get in the way of a good story. Apparently this woman maintained a vice-like grip on a small coin despite every attempt that people made to persuade her to give it up. However, when she died some mean-minded member of staff stole it and she was therefore buried without her talisman. The screams are those of this former inmate whose ghost is presumably looking for the coin or trying to settle accounts with the person who stole it.

Broad Street Station of the North London Railway was opened by 1865 adjacent to where the Great Eastern Railway Co. later opened its Liverpool Street Station. The building of Broad Street had required the disposal of huge numbers of human remains from a burial ground which stood in the way. Among the occupants had been John Lilburne (*c.*1614-1657), the radical political agitator who rose to prominence in the English Civil War, and Lodowick Muggleton (1609-1698), who founded a religious sect which he modestly named after himself and who argued, among other things, that the Devil became incarnate in Eve. They never had many adherents (although the last known Muggletonian, Philip Noakes, died in the late 1970s).

In 1911-1912 engineers working on an extension of the Central London Railway came across densely packed masses of bones in the vicinity of Liverpool Street Station. Some years earlier, a passenger waiting for a train at Broad Street Station reported that a newspaper boy had casually asked him when he bought his paper if he would like a human skeleton as well.

Is it not possible that the reports of horrible screaming heard around this complex of platforms and lines relate to one or more of the inmates of the nearby burial grounds, who are responding in the only way they know how to the disturbance of their resting place?

MAIDA VALE

As late as the early nineteenth century, Maida Vale was farmland with a few wooded areas and the occasional farmhouse. In the nineteenth century smart villas in sizeable grounds began to appear. The district began to be intensively developed for housing in the second half of the nineteenth century and by 1900 the mansion blocks which characterise Maida Vale were appearing, especially along the main arterial roads. In 1915 the Bakerloo Line Station opened, a tube station of course but actually built above ground.

Nothing of the visible kind manifests itself at Maida Vale tube. However, there have been several witnesses who have talked about feeling invisible hands apparently placing their own hands onto the handrails as they have been coming up the escalators from platform to street level. The grip has been a firm one, pressing the hands down onto the rail but the feeling this strange sensation evokes is apparently not a fearful one. Rather, it is as if the person is being carefully and solicitously guided or steered for his or her own benefit.

MARBLE ARCH

Marble Arch on the deep-level tube Central London Railway opened on 30 July 1900. The line proved an immediate success with its passengers and quickly gained the nickname the 'Twopenny Tube', the twopenny flat fare proving to be a great draw. The Central London Railway can justifiably be described as the first modern tube line.

There is talk of a mysterious figure at Marble Arch who rides up, but never down, the escalator. In 1973 a lady passenger alighted at platform level and then made her way in leisurely fashion towards the exit – she was in no hurry. It was a quiet time of the day and she was the last person to alight from the train and the last onto the escalator. Letting the escalator move her, she was nearly at the top when she became uneasy, aware of a figure that had noiselessly stolen up right behind her. Not liking to turn her head round completely, out of the corner of her eye she saw what she described as a man all in black, with a trilby and long, expensive-looking overcoat. His presence so close behind her was menacing. She looked ahead again as she moved off the escalator but then, succumbing to the need to satisfy her curiosity, she turned round again for a proper look. The figure had vanished! As she plunged into the comforting melee of people outside the station in Oxford Street, she knew

Maida Vale Station. Watch out for the feel of an invisible hand as you hold the handrail on the escalator.

someone or something had been there, but she was left wondering where it had come from and where it had gone.

Other users of the Central Line have had a similar experience at Marble Arch – always at times when the station is fairly quiet.

Marble Arch stands close to the spot where at least 50,000 people met their deaths between the twelfth century and 1783. This was Tyburn, London's main place of public execution. Hanging days at Tyburn attracted huge crowds who came for the free entertainment provided by hearing the last dying speeches of the condemned felons and watching them in their death agonies. Those who were popular criminals and who went to their deaths with courage or even defiance were cheered by the crowds. Those found guilty of crimes that were disapproved of or who were visibly terrified of the ordeal they were about to undergo were scoffed at and abused. Although the bodies of some of those who met their death at Tyburn were taken away to be used by the surgeons for demonstration purposes, countless numbers were placed in unmarked burial pits close by and their remains have been unearthed from time to time during building work. It is believed that the body of Oliver Cromwell was among those unceremoniously dumped in one of these pits – minus its head, of course. A head said to be Cromwell's is interred in a wall at Sidney Sussex College Chapel, Cambridge. The mystery of exactly what happened to Cromwell's head is a conundrum which has fascinated historians and others for centuries.

Large numbers of expensive flats and opulent mansions cluster around the Marble Arch and have views over the north-east corner of Hyde Park where the Tyburn scaffold and gallows stood. The

Station totem or name board at platform level. These familiar icons have developed over more than a century and the last time any alteration was made to the design was in 1972. Have any readers had spooky experiences leaving the platforms at Marble Arch and making their way up the escalators?

exact spot is not known. Perhaps it is not surprising that there have been a number of reports from these affluent residents of the sounds of boisterous cheering and jeering. More striking have been the re-enactments they claim to have seen. These involve large crowds milling around the scaffold, always apparently dressed in the clothes of the eighteenth century. These apparitions, which are usually seen early in the morning, are fleeting and are followed by the appearance of mist.

MOORGATE

In 1415 the wall of the City of London was pierced to make the Moor Gate at a spot which edged a tract of somewhat marshy country called Moorfields. The idea was that the gate would improve communications via causeways to and from Islington and Hoxton. The gate was demolished in 1762. Moorgate Street, as it was then known, was built in the 1830s as part of a route connecting the City with London Bridge. The first trains started running to a station in Moorgate in 1865 when the Metropolitan Railway was extended from what is now Farringdon.

Moorgate is a complicated Underground station. The sub-surface trains of the Circle, Metropolitan and Hammersmith & City Lines call at Moorgate, as do the tube trains on the Northern Line's route via Bank. It hosts, in two entirely different parts of the station, National Rail trains currently operated by First Capital Connect. These provide services terminating at such places as Hertford North and Letchworth Garden City and also, during peak periods, trains to Bedford via St Albans and Luton. As far as King's Cross the latter travel over what used to be called 'The Widened Lines'.

Those trains travelling to Hertford and Letchworth run along the tracks of the former Great Northern and City Railway as far as Finsbury Park. This was built as a tube railway but was unusual in being constructed to the main-line loading gauge. This route came to be known as the Northern City Line, having become part of the Northern Line in 1939. The northern terminus was cut back to Drayton Park in 1964. In the early 1970s, plans were afoot for the electrification of the British

Moorgate Station.

Railways suburban services out of King's Cross and Moorgate and this included the Northern City Line. Late in 1975 this line was brought into the main-line system and converted to the overhead electricity pick-up system. The Northern City Line part of the station was the scene of the worst-ever accident involving a train on London's Underground. The reason why the disaster occurred has never been satisfactorily established.

What happened was this. Just after a quarter to nine on the morning of 28 February 1975, a southbound train entered the terminal platform No. 9 without showing signs of decelerating and crashed at about 40mph into a thick concrete wall marking, literally, the end of the line. A massive rescue and recovery operation was launched, working in appallingly hot and confined conditions. It took over four days to bring all the bodies out. Forty-three people died; seventy-four were seriously injured.

Driver Newson was an experienced, conscientious and reliable man, known to be, if anything, ultra-cautious in his approach to work and absolutely scrupulous about observing all speed restrictions. The entrance to the platform at Moorgate had a 15mph speed limit. The driver had died in the crash, and immediately speculation erupted to the effect that he had been under the influence of drink or drugs or had fallen asleep at the controls. Taking pressure off the ominously named dead man's handle would, of course, have brought the train to a swift halt. Was he bent on committing suicide and had he decided to take the train and its passengers with him? Tests on Newson revealed nothing untoward – nothing in his life outside work suggested a troubled mind. Nor was any technical fault found with the train or the signalling equipment.

Seconds before the crash eyewitnesses said that they had seen him in his cab, upright and looking fixedly ahead, apparently unaware of the wall of death towards which he was careering in such a headlong fashion. The verdict was accidental death and the official inquiry found that the accident was solely caused by a lapse on the part of the driver. If this was the correct verdict then what caused the lapse in the first place?

The mysteries surrounding this appalling catastrophe led some people to seek a paranormal explanation. Did Driver Newson see an apparition? As soon as discussion around this kind of possibility started, it was probably inevitable that people would appear announcing that they had seen ghosts in this part of Moorgate Station. Others declared that the station had a history of hauntings and strange apparitions. Certainly, during the winter of 1974-1975 and shortly before the disaster, a gang of engineers on the night shift in the Northern City tunnels at the approach to Moorgate saw a figure in blue overalls approaching them. As it got nearer they saw that his face bore a look of appalled horror but before they could see him too closely, he vanished. They thought that the apparition was that of a line-maintenance worker who had been run down and killed by a train on this stretch of line some time earlier.

When this incident came to light, some 'explained' the disaster by saying that Driver Newson must have seen this apparition and been so startled that he momentarily lost concentration. Others said that the ghost the men saw earlier was a premonition of the impending disaster.

Moorgate First Capital Connect suburban platform, formerly Northern Line and scene of the Underground's worst disaster.

QUEENSBURY

The Metropolitan Railway opened its branch line to Stanmore late in 1932. About two years later Queensbury Station opened, at first a very basic shanty-like building. The route was transferred to the Bakerloo Line in 1939 and then became part of the Jubilee Line in 1979. Queensbury is a perfect example of the suburbs which sprang up so quickly in the inter-war years. In this case much of the development took place on what had previously been an aircraft factory and associated airfield belonging to the De Havilland Co.

In the 1980s a sensation was caused when reports came in that the figure of Sir Winston Churchill had been seen on the platform at Queensbury, apparently waiting for a train. Disappointingly it was never reported whether or not he actually got on the train. Churchill, who had died in 1965, was no devotee of public transport so the idea that his spirit was lurking around the Bakerloo Line seemed a trifle unlikely. However, it could be explained by the fact that apparently he once lived nearby.

Statue of Winston Churchill in Parliament Square. Made of bronze, it was unveiled in 1973.

'The Allies'. Unveiled in 1995 to commemorate fifty years of peace since the Second World War, this sculpture shows Sir Winston Churchill and US President Franklin D. Roosevelt in relaxed and chatty mode. This work can be seen in New Bond Street.

RICKMANSWORTH

Rickmansworth, or 'Ricky' as it known to its aficionados, was a small and little-known market town of ancient origins when the Metropolitan Railway arrived in 1887. A few well-to-do people making their livelihood in London built their villas there over the next thirty years but it was in the 1920s and 1930s that Rickmansworth blossomed and grew – never too fast – as a model for 'Metroland'. It drew well-paid professional and mercantile men who wished to combine the financial and other advantages that employment in a world city brought with residence in a socially exclusive and sylvan near-rural neighbourhood which nevertheless had quick and easy rail access to central London.

Trains from Baker Street approaching Rickmansworth pass a substantial fan of sidings used for stabling rolling stock on the north side of the line. These are known as the 'South Sidings'. Rail workers have long reckoned that one of the stabling roads in these sidings is haunted. Over the years, threatening noises have been heard and invisible but menacing presences sensed on this particular siding. Train crew waiting for signals to leave the sidings and take up service have heard carriage doors slide open and close but without human agency. Occasionally an indistinct figure is seen out of the corner of an eye. Stories circulate that the sidings are built over the site of an ancient monastery but research does not confirm this. What then is the cause of these disquieting experiences?

SOUTH KENSINGTON

This stylish district contains a collection of museums built on land bought with profits from the Great Exhibition which was held in nearby Hyde Park in 1851. Prince Albert had been a major supporter of this highly successful international trade fair and after he died in 1861, the Albert

Memorial and Albert Hall were erected in his memory. With some degree of irony, the district around Exhibition Road with its museums and places of learning gained the informal name 'Albertopolis'. The residential parts of South Kensington are characterised by up-market terraces of white stuccoed four- or five-storey mansions. There are many French eating places and French cultural events taking place in this area.

South Kensington opened in 1868 as an intermediate station on the sub-surface line operated by the Metropolitan Railway from Gloucester Road to Westminster. In 1871 trains of the Metropolitan District Railway also began to call. In 1907 platforms were opened on the deep-level tube Great Northern, Piccadilly and Brompton Railway. The station is now served by the Circle, District and Piccadilly Lines.

The rather scanty details of an underground ghost relate to a sighting in 1928 in the sub-surface part of South Kensington Station. A passenger alighting from the last train found himself alone on the platform whereupon he reported having seen a spectral steam locomotive on the track with the figure of a man standing next to it. So far, so good. The next bit is puzzling. According to the witness both locomotive and human figure then vanished into the covered way close by. Since this had no rails, this is somewhat puzzling. What did he see?

STOCKWELL

Stockwell is a district of London south of the Thames which can aptly be described as 'cosmopolitan'. The station opened as the southern terminus of the City & South London Railway tube in 1890. In 1900 this line was extended to Clapham Common and in 1926 to Morden. In 1971 Stockwell became an interchange station when the Victoria Line to Brixton began to operate.

The Northern Line northwards from Stockwell towards Oval is reputedly haunted by a figure looking like an old-fashioned workman. It is believed to be the ghost of a track worker who was killed by a train on this stretch of line sometime in the 1950s.

TURNHAM GREEN

The origins of Turnham Green Station lie with the London and South Western Railway. The shenanigans of the politics of London's early railway promotion and building are extremely complicated but keeping it as simple as possible, the L & SWR came to a mutually helpful agreement with the long-forgotten North & South Western Junction Railway to build a line from the latter's Addison Road, now Kensington Olympia Station, to Richmond. This line opened for passengers in 1869. In 1874, after an extension had joined Hammersmith to this line near the present Ravenscourt Park, District Line trains bound for Richmond began to serve Turnham Green. In 1879 District Line trains to Ealing Broadway also started calling.

The station is on a viaduct and located a couple of hundred yards away from Chiswick High Street and it is near Chiswick Park and also Bedford Park. The latter can be described as London's first garden suburb and was built between 1875 and 1881. Much of Chiswick is chic and for many years it has been a bustling, affluent suburb and a highly desirable address. On the face of it Chiswick would not seem to be very propitious territory for the supernatural. However, less than ten years ago there were a number of sightings of what was described as a 'semi-transparent' apparition walking by

South Kensington Station, where a special steam locomotive was seen.

the side of the four-track section of line close to the station. A number of people saw it on different occasions and said that it was dark grey and wore a knee-length cape. Apparently it vanished if the witness looked away for a second. The only way to gain access to the track at the station would be to walk off the end of the platform, too risky an enterprise for most people but for a ghost – who knows? Can something disembodied be electrocuted? We wait with bated breath for the first ghost to be seen walking the line wearing high-visibility clothing.

Chiswick was actually an ancient Thameside fishing village with a church which was originally founded in the twelfth century; the area has several ghosts. Chiswick House boasts the ghost of the Duchess of Cleveland, one of the many mistresses of Charles II. The King was affectionately known, among other things, as 'The Merry Monarch'. He was a compulsive philanderer, a fact which gained him another admiring nickname. This was 'Old Rowley'. The original Old Rowley was an ancient goat, known far and wide for being exceptionally randy, who was familiar to tens of thousands of Londoners because for years he was tethered close to the Palace of Westminster.

Other Chiswick hauntings include the ghost of a woman murdered in the late eighteenth century in a building which has subsequently been used as a fire station and then a police station. In 1956 a council house in Chiswick hit the headlines because of the poltergeist activity that was apparently taking place there. The Old Burlington pub claims to have been a favoured watering hole of Dick Turpin. The ghost who wears a wide-brimmed black hat and long cloak may have been an

Left: Stockwell on the Northern Line looking towards Oval and the haunted stretch.

Below: Turnham Green platforms looking westwards.

Turnham Green looking towards Hammersmith. A ghost in severe danger of electrocution?

associate of Dick Turpin. Chiswick Warehouse, a huge furniture depository, contained a number of exceptionally cold areas with a menacing atmosphere which the employees were always unwilling to tarry in unless they absolutely had to.

VAUXHALL

The Victoria Line took a long time coming. Plans had existed for this line as long ago as the 1940s but it only received parliamentary sanction in 1962. Most of the line opened in March 1969 and the extension south to Brixton on which Vauxhall is located opened in 1971. The engineers constructing the line encountered serious problems in the vicinity owing to the waterlogged nature of the soil and had to freeze it before it could be excavated.

Vauxhall was famous for its pleasure gardens which dated back to the seventeenth century and were revamped in 1785, acting as a model for similar parks in several continental cities. They closed in 1859 by which time they had become shabby and disreputable, although they had once been exclusive and fashionable. In the nineteenth century the district became intensively industrialised and among the businesses was the Vauxhall Ironworks Co., which started building cars in 1903, relocated to Luton in 1905 and then took the name 'Vauxhall Motors' in 1907.

While the line was being built, a mysterious figure described as being 7ft tall, wearing brown overalls and a cloth cap was seen on a number of occasions in the workings. At that height, he was bound to be a bit scary but he never allowed any of the bolder building workers to get too close to

Vauxhall Station, where a mysterious 7ft-tall figure was seen by workmen during the building of the line in 1968.

him. This ghost became eminent enough to have an article devoted to it in an edition of *The People* in December 1968. No conclusions were ever reached about who or what he was or what he was doing down there. If he was seen today, doubtless Health and Safety would hound him relentlessly to ensure that he put on a hard hat and high-visibility clothing.

WEST BROMPTON

This station opened on 12 April 1869. At first it was the terminus of a service of the Metropolitan District Railway from Gloucester Road Station which made use of running powers over the West London Extension Railway. This line was extended to Wimbledon in 1889.

Now part of the Borough of Kensington and Chelsea, some parts of Brompton are extremely fashionable. However, typically of London, not all of Brompton's inhabitants regard themselves as the up and coming set and there are pockets of poverty and deprivation cheek by jowl with parts where conspicuous consumption is regarded as *de rigeur* by the well-heeled residents. The urban development of this part of London took place rapidly in the nineteenth century. Before that time the area consisted of fairly marginal agricultural land and containing a lot of market gardens to serve the vast demand provided by London so close by.

Fans of such things consider Brompton Cemetery to be one of the London's finest. It opened for business in 1840. It is now closed for additional interments except where old tombs are reopened

Above: West Brompton from the footbridge looking south towards Wimbledon on the District Line.

Right: Brompton Cemetery.

Side elevation and Leslie Green design work in Cottage Place SW3. Brompton Road Station on the Piccadilly Line closed in 1932. This station was always poorly used and was replaced when new exits were built at nearby Knightsbridge Station.

for new occupants to be laid to rest. About 200,000 people have been buried in this cemetery. The inmates include many winners of the Victoria Cross: Sir Samuel Cunard (1787-1865), who founded the Cunard Steam Packet Co. in 1840; Jonathan Holt (1820-1887), who claimed fame on the basis of being the first Bishop of Rangoon; Percy Lambert (1881-1913), the first man recorded as having driven a car at over 100mph and who was eventually killed at Brooklands, perhaps not unexpectedly, given that he was trying to go even faster; Henry Mears, who died in 1912 and was a builder and the founder of Chelsea Football Club; Emmeline Pankhurst (1858-1928), the militant suffragette; and Samuel Smiles (1812-1904), the rather smug author of *Self-Help* which was a compilation of brief biographies of 'great men'.

The curious traveller will find the cemetery adjacent to West Brompton Underground Station. You could almost fall out of one into the other. Perhaps it is this proximity which has something to do with the ghost which has been seen at the station by many people and on many occasions although, apparently, only early in the morning and late at night, times when the station is not at its most frequented. He strides purposefully along the platform, looking for all the world just as you would expect a workman of the late Victorian or Edwardian period to look. However, as soon as the witnesses rub their eyes to make sure of what they are seeing, he vanishes.

4

OTHER HAUNTINGS

BAKERLOO LINE

In the vicinity of Elephant and Castle and various other Bakerloo Line stations, especially Baker Street, there have many reports from passengers who were sitting and gazing into space only to look up and catch a glimpse of the reflection of another passenger sitting next to them. This would be all well and good except that the passengers making these reports were sitting at the time with unoccupied seats on either side of them. The vast majority of such reports concern trains going northwards.

The Bakerloo is not unique in producing this strange phenomenon but none of the other lines can compete with it for the number of occasions on which travellers have had this rather disconcerting experience. The nearest rival seems to be the Piccadilly Line near Earl's Court.

A variation on this theme is for the reflection to be that of a figure dressed in the clothes of a bygone era. What is to be made of that?

JUBILEE LINE

Since the Underground began being built in the nineteenth century, old burial grounds have been disrupted and the bones of the dead disturbed. In more recent times one such disruption has been that of the Cross Bones burial ground at Redcross Way, between London Bridge Station and Borough Station. The burial ground was excavated by archaeologists between 1991 and 1998 as a result of the extension to the Jubilee Line.

The Cross Bones graveyard lies behind a vacant plot of land enclosed by London Underground boards. Building work in the 1920s led to the exhumation of many bones, as did work in the 1990s for a new substation for the Jubilee Line. The report *The Cross Bones Burial Ground* (Museum of London Archaeological Service 1999) and excavation was conducted by MoLAS on the medieval burial ground. It provided a final resting place for the poor of St Saviour's Parish in Southwark. The parish supported several burial grounds including Deadman's Place (now Park Street) which was originally used for the interment of large numbers of victims of the plague.

The gates to the Cross Bones burial ground, Redcross Way Southwark.

Mementos placed on the gates of Cross Bones burial ground.

Cross Bones Graveyard

In medieval times this was an unconsecrated graveyard for prostitutes or 'Winchester Geese'. By the 18th century it had become a paupers' burial ground, which closed in 1853. Here, local people have created a memorial shrine.

The Outcast Dead R.I.P

Above: A plaque at Cross Bones graveyard noting the reference to the 'Winchester Geese' – prostitutes who lived and worked from houses owned by the Bishop of Winchester.

Right: Notice on the gates of Cross Bones graveyard requesting respect for the thousands of dead buried there.

Here is the site of an ancient burial ground

The shrine on these gates honours up to 15,000 people buried in the Cross Bones graveyard on this site. Many of their names are lost in the mists of time. We have not forgotten them.

Please respect this shrine!

The area around Southwark and Bankside was well know for its 'stews' or brothels and London historian John Stow (1525–1605) wrote in 1603 that the graveyard was used for 'single women' – prostitutes referred to at the time as 'Winchester Geese' because they lived in and operated from dwellings owned by the Bishop of Winchester. Many graveyards became prey to the activities of the resurrection men – body snatchers – and Cross Bones was no exception. These men would steal freshly buried bodies and sell them to surgeons who sought specimens for their anatomy classes at nearby Guy's Hospital. By the nineteenth century the area was overcrowded and disease infested as well as a popular haunt for criminals. Not surprisingly many paupers were interred in the burial ground. It was closed in 1853 because it was not only overcrowded but also a threat to public health.

Archaeologists from MoLAS eventually removed 148 skeletons – only a small fraction (less than 1 per cent) of those buried at this site. The bodies were piled on top of each other with most buried in cheap coffins in the ill kept and unconsecrated burial ground.

As more sites are disturbed increased sightings of ghosts are reported, particularly accounts of phantom monks walking the tracks have begun to emerge. However, attempts are made to respect the remains of the dead in such burial sites. For example Southwark Council were refused planning permission in 2002 for three office blocks to be erected on the graveyard and future plans hope that an area will be reserved to serve as a Cross Bones memorial park.

Another excavation was the Cistercian monastery of St Mary Stratford Langthorne which once stood on land south of the new Jubilee Line station at Stratford. The site of the old abbey, which was all but destroyed in the dissolution of the monasteries between 1536 and 1540, now lies under the Jubilee Line. 647 burials were found in the cemetery. The Black Death struck the abbey in the fourteenth century. Excavations between 1973 and 1994 recorded large parts of the cemetery as well as the monastic church. The skeletons found were in shallow graves and, prior to the building of the Jubilee Line, a number of Cistercian monks from Sutton Coldfield in the West Midlands removed some of the bones for reburial at the Sutton Coldfield Abbey.

5

CLOSED RAILWAY STATIONS

The mainline railway network of Greater London is one of extraordinary complexity. Compared to the system in the provinces, London's railways have escaped relatively unscathed from the welter of line and station closures which began in the First World War, continued intermittently through the 1950s and then surged in the 1960s and 1970s, only to become thankfully much more intermittent since that time.

There is something poignant about stations on which the lights have gone out for ever, about track formations whose rails have been uprooted but where the impressions of the sleepers can still be seen, about railway viaducts that no longer carry trains, long-forgotten goods depots or even about rusted rails stretching into the distance through luxuriously rampant vegetation, never to witness the passing of another train.

It is easy for us to imagine that the men and women who worked in these places, the passengers that went to and fro and perhaps even the trains themselves return in spectral form to the places with which they were once so familiar.

There are a myriad of such sites in London. Those with a liking for ghosts, railways and industrial archaeology could make intelligent use of maps and reference books and find many places that would reward exploration. A few suggestions might include the Seven Sisters to Palace Gates branch of the Great Eastern Railway, the branch from Nunhead to Greenwich Park, traces of the London, Chatham and Dover Line from Nunhead to Crystal Palace High Level, the mothballed line between Epping and Ongar or the London & North Western Railway's branch line from Harrow & Wealdstone to Stanmore Village. We can be sure that these and many similar places have their ghosts!

CRYSTAL PALACE

The district around Crystal Palace is deep in that enclave of south London that has never been served by the London Underground system. It did, however, have an underground railway of sorts and a particularly interesting one. There have been reported sightings of ghosts associated with this railway.

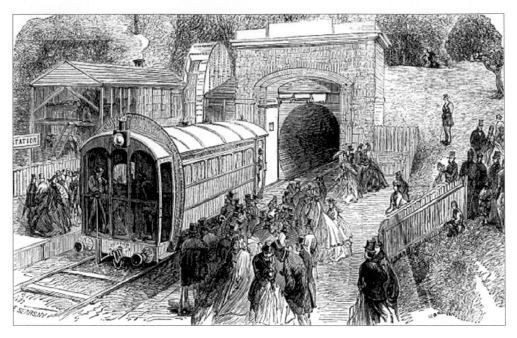

Crystal Palace pneumatic railway in 1864.

The Great Exhibition was held in Hyde Park in London in 1851. It was an international trade fair set up by the British for two main reasons. Firstly, it was a showcase for the products of British manufacturing industry which was then rightly thought of as being the 'Workshop of the World'. It was hoped that it would boost Britain's already burgeoning export trade. Secondly, and rather naively, it was hoped that bringing the nations of the world together as trading partners in a spirit of mutual amity might reduce the possibilities of future wars. The Great Exhibition was considered an enormous success at the time and unexpectedly huge numbers of visitors flocked from all parts of Britain and many overseas places to enjoy the spectacle.

The exhibition was housed in a striking and highly innovative prefabricated building made largely of glass and iron and inspirationally nicknamed 'The Crystal Palace'. Londoners and others took the Crystal Palace to their hearts and wanted it to stay in Hyde Park as a permanent fixture. However, this was impossible under the terms governing the staging of the exhibition and it was quickly dismantled. The pieces were stored but eventually a consortium of what would now be called 'venture capitalists' re-erected an enlarged version of the building at Sydenham Hill to be an exhibition hall, the centrepiece of an amusement and entertainment complex. The district round about quickly came to be known as 'Crystal Palace'.

It proved to be a great attraction for several decades. In 1864, about ten years after the relocation of the Crystal Palace, an experimental demonstration 'pneumatic' railway was built in the grounds. This was a development of Isambard Kingdom Brunel's unsuccessful atmospheric railway in south Devon. A passenger carriage ran on a broad gauge track for a distance of 600yds through a tunnel, quickly and silently. A return fare, expensive at 6d a time, proved no deterrent to those who wanted to sample this novel form of propulsion. The success of this small-scale operation encouraged a company to propose what would have been London's first tube railway. It would have run from Whitehall to Waterloo and work even began on the building of the tube tunnel but was abandoned because of the financial crisis of 1866. The stub of this tunnel is apparently still in situ.

In due course the 'pneumatic' railway closed but before long a myth developed that the carriage remained within the bricked-up tunnel and contained a grisly cargo of skeletal forgotten passengers. These physical human remains may have been unable to do anything about their predicament but their accompanying spirits were apparently highly indignant about being immured in this way and were waiting to exact revenge from the living.

Traces of this tunnel could be seen for many years and in the early 1990s an edition of the *New Civil Engineer* carried an article with photographs taken many years earlier inside the tunnel. No abandoned carriage containing equally abandoned skeletons was to be seen and if there were ghosts, they had kept themselves to themselves. According to the article, no trace of the tunnel survived. This has not prevented occasional reports of spectres in the vicinity. The site of the Crystal Palace is, after all, a place of ghostly memories.

6

Defunct Underground Stations

On the Underground system between 1 a.m. and 5 a.m. the current is switched off and an army of maintenance workers descend on the system to ensure that the next day's services will be punctual and safe. The safety record and quality of service is evidence of what a good job these hidden and unsung heroes do.

However, in the labyrinth of tunnels, platforms, stairways, passages, sidings and shunting necks that make up the system, can we be sure that there are not other creatures of the night? Rats galore there are of course, but could there be other entities, living or some perhaps deceased, that become active when the last passengers have been excluded for the night? Many stations have tunnels and passages that are sealed off from public use. What creatures may lurk in them?

Even more propitious for hauntings by who-knows-what are the closed stations on the system. There is evidence of several of these at street level while some traces of former platforms can be seen by those with a quick eye who know where to look. Among former stations with substantial remaining evidence at street level are Aldwych, York Road, South Kentish Town and Brompton Road. Just visible from passing trains are parts of such stations as St Mary's (Whitechapel Road), York Road, British Museum and City Road.

Perhaps the most fascinating closed station is one that never opened. This was the putative 'North End' which has come to be thought of as 'Bull and Bush'. It would have been on what became the Northern Line, breaking up the lengthy section between Golders Green and Hampstead. There was little housing close by when the line was mooted and, by the time trains were running in 1907, it had been decided not to proceed with the development of North End Station although the platforms and a few associated passages had been built. There was no access to the surface.

North End was an extremely deep station and it was used during the Second World War for the safe storage of vital archives. The only way to get to refer to this material when necessary was to make an arrangement for the archivist to travel in the cab with the driver who would then let him off at the uncompleted platform at North End. The feelings of this person as the lighted train from which he had just stepped rushed away into the tunnel can well be imagined. There were rudimentary lights but, except when trains approached and passed, there was a pervasive, tangible and absolute cold silence and loneliness. However, it would have been too easy to start imagining that they were not after all entirely alone and that slimy things were crawling with slimy legs towards them, full of malign intent. The hours must have weighed heavily. What would have happened to the poor archivist if the instructions had been misunderstood and the appointed hour passed and no train stopped to pick him up?

York Road Station.

7

'GHOST' STEAM TRAINS

The last standard gauge steam locomotives were withdrawn from British Railways in August 1968. Steam-hauled passenger trains on the Metropolitan Line had ended in 1961 but London Transport had, for a long time, used a small fleet of steam locomotives on engineers' and various other departmental trains on the sub-surface lines. Three steam duties continued until June 1971. They were all based at London Transport's Lillie Bridge depot near Earl's Court. One ran during daylight hours to Acton Yard while the others were nocturnal return trips to Neasden via Rayners Lane and Upminster via the District Line through Victoria, Whitechapel and Barking. The locomotives concerned were ex-Great Western Railway pannier tanks of a class originally introduced in 1929. Typically London Transport kept them in a very smart condition. These departmental trains had always been rather shy and secretive, many of them operating at night when the passenger trains had stopped running.

The ending of mainline steam trains had received extensive coverage in the media of the time but no sooner had this happened than stories started circulating that there were ghost trains on the London Underground! The unmistakeable sound and smell of steam locomotives at work in the witching hours, the occasional mournful whistle and the trails of smoke they made, emanating from parts of the system open to the elements but often hidden from view behind hoardings and below street level, all came together to create a new piece of London folklore. Ghostly steam trains were at large on the Underground!

The fact that similar departmental workings had been taking place for decades was conveniently ignored. These steam locomotives had been puffing around on such largely nocturnal and unglamorous duties for years, largely unnoticed or not remarked about. However, hadn't the media told everyone that steam locomotives were a thing of the past? Therefore they must be ghosts!

Every so often since the 1970s there have been reports of a ghostly steam locomotive which manifests itself on the Northern Line between East Finchley Station and the nearby Wellington Sidings.

GIPSY HILL TO CRYSTAL PALACE

The stretch of line between Gipsy Hill and Crystal Palace belonged to the West End of London & Crystal Palace Railway Co., but it was operated from its opening in 1856 by the London, Brighton & South Coast Railway and eventually subsumed within the latter's system.

This part of south London is very hilly and between the two stations the line runs through Crystal Palace Tunnel. This tunnel is reputed to be haunted. Many years ago a track-maintenance worker was run down and killed by a train in the tunnel. He was decapitated in the process. His ghost has been seen on many occasions wandering disconsolately around the tunnel apparently engaged in the search for its missing head. Unfortunately those who have witnessed the ghost's underground peregrinations have omitted to say whether or not the ghost appeared to be headless.

HADLEY WOOD TUNNEL

Hadley Wood is in the leafy and undulating area north of New Barnet. It has a station on the East Coast Main Line served only by suburban trains. The line opened in 1850 but the few inhabitants of what was then a scattered rural community had to wait until 1885 before the then Great Northern Railway provided a station. This was built largely in anticipation that the station would attract house building nearby as they so often did.

The station is in a cutting and between tunnels. For a time the double track through Hadley Wood had been a considerable bottleneck, and eventually, in 1959, the line at this point was quadrupled. The tunnels go by the simple names of Hadley Wood North and Hadley Wood South.

Some people believe that Hadley Wood South Tunnel is haunted by a ghostly diesel locomotive. This is D9020, later known as No. 55020 and named *Nimbus* after a classic racehorse. The Deltics were hated at first by railway enthusiasts as this class of twenty-two locomotives replaced fifty-five steam locomotives including many magnificent Gresley Pacifics. In time, however, even many of the most hardened steam buffs came to admire the 'Deltics'. They packed a real punch, having two 18-cylinder Napier engines and they used to tear up and down the East Coast Main Line on the heaviest and fastest expresses.

Nimbus was withdrawn from traffic around 1980 but, if the stories are to be believed, it could not bear to leave the East Coast Main Line. The authors have been unable to ascertain whether it has been seen moving or simply lurking in the tunnel. Enthusiasts will remember the characteristic roar that these locomotives made especially when accelerating from a stand. A tunnel haunted by one of these locomotives making that roar would satisfy even the most demanding railway ghost hunter.

HOLBORN TO CHANCERY LANE

The Central London Railway opened in 1900. In the 1960s and 1970s many motormen dreaded being held up by signals on the section between these two stations. This is not surprising given that many of these workers, by no means the most fanciful people in the world, reported that when their trains drew to a halt at adverse signals, they would suddenly become aware that, in the partial light shed by the carriage lights behind them, they were sharing the driving cab with an uninvited guest. This indistinct figure was apparently staring fixedly ahead through the cab's front windows and standing just a foot or two away from them. As soon as the train moved off when the signals changed, the figure vanished.

Whatever it was, this phenomenon was sufficiently threatening for a number of motormen to travel as slowly as possible between the two stations, anxiously hoping that by doing so, they would not have to stop for signals.

KINGSWAY TRAM TUNNEL

Kingsway was conceived in the 1900s in conjunction with New Oxford Street, Shaftesbury Avenue and Charing Cross Road as one of a tranche of new roads built to ease congestion and to help to eliminate some of London's most notorious slum areas often referred to as 'criminal rookeries'. Kingsway opened in 1905 and the Kingsway Tram Tunnel in 1906. It was extended to the Victoria Embankment in 1908 and acted as a link between the north and south London tram systems. At first it was used only by single-deck trams but it was enlarged in 1931 after which double-deckers could operate through it. Three tram routes ran through the tunnel between Embankment and Theobalds Road. Londoners affectionately referred to the Kingsway Tram Tunnel as 'The Spout'. Part of the northern exit to the tunnel was on a gradient of 1 in 10 and this provided a stern test for the skills of the tram driver and his vehicle's traction motors.

The tunnel had two intermediate tram stations at Holborn and Aldwych. These were immensely atmospheric places, not very far below ground. They had white tiled walls to reflect and maximise the light and were something like a combination of a tube and a sub-surface underground station while yet being distinctly different. In the 1930s, 1940s and early 1950s London was still afflicted by 'pea-souper' smogs and the almost tangible murk that resulted permeated easily into these stations, filling them with an almost impenetrable air of eerie mystery. Between the arrival and departure of the trams, the smog rendered the stations extraordinarily quiet given their location in the heart of the Metropolis. The silence was only broken by the hiss of the enormous gas lamps which provided the illumination, which under the conditions gave off a fuzzy glow.

The favourite uncle of one of the authors used the Aldwych Tram Station on a regular daily basis. He was a great fan of Surrey County Cricket Club and spent many happy hours watching his heroes at the Oval. There he struck up a close friendship with another cricket fan, a milkman who had moved to London from recession-hit South Wales in the 1930s. They both lived in London but in districts some distance apart and they renewed their friendship at the beginning of each cricket season.

Going to work one morning in the winter, he was at Aldwych Tram Station when he was surprised to see his old friend coming down the platform towards him with what he described as 'a fixed expression' on his face. He stepped forward to greet him only for his friend to pass him by with no sign of recognition. He was puzzled and not a little put out. Next day exactly the same thing happened. The uncle was quite hurt – it was just not like his friend because he always had a cheery word for everyone. However, he was already late for work and had to hurry on. When he got home, a letter was waiting for him. It was from his friend's widow. It described how he had been knocked down and killed by a tram on another part of the system the day before he made the first of his two appearances at Aldwych Tram Station.

Surviving tram lines at the northern end of Kingsway Tram Tunnel. Remarkable survivors given that trams stopped running in 1952!

The last trams ran in London in April 1952 and obviously the Kingsway Tram Tunnel closed. In 1964 part of it was converted into a traffic underpass. The rest of the tunnel is still there. In recent years Transport for London has considered restoring trams to the streets of the capital but has apparently ruled out reusing the Kingsway Tram Tunnel for this purpose.

LONDON ROAD DEPOT

Few of the travelling public know of the existence of the London Road depot of the Bakerloo Line. It stands near to St George's Circus in the Lambeth district south of the Thames. It was originally the engineering works for the Bakerloo Line rolling stock as well as being the line's major stabling point. It opened when the Bakerloo Line services started early in March 1906. It is hidden away from prying eyes below street level but is open to the elements. Its access to the Bakerloo main line is through a single-line tube tunnel close to Lambeth North station. The depot remains in use for stabling rolling stock.

Bakerloo line staff have provided many reports of strange noises and unexplained appearances around the depot and most especially in the connecting tunnel. In the sidings in the small hours of the morning repeated metallic-sounding tapping noises have been heard as if an old-fashioned wheeltapper was at work. This has happened on innumerable occasions at times when no maintenance work was being done on the carriages. More disturbing have been the shadowy figures seen passing hither and thither in the sidings and often disappearing into the entrance tunnel. Witnesses have never managed to get a good look at them – the apparitions keep their distance and have been described as 'blurred round the edges'. The appearance of these figures is apparently more disconcerting and puzzling than actually menacing. Was there a burial pit in the vicinity which was disturbed when the Bakerloo Line was built?

Another apparition in the area is that of a nun. She is thought to have been connected with a nearby convent school.

Above: London Road depot of the Bakerloo Line.

Left: Greenford Station. Between here and Northolt on the Central Line, sightings of a large puma-like creature have been reported.

NORTHOLT TO GREENFORD

In the 1990s there were reports that a puma or, even more extraordinarily, the ghost of a puma had been seen on the Central Line between Northolt and Greenford. This section of the line runs on the surface.

Over the years and from many parts of Britain there have been significant numbers of reported sightings of 'big' cats. Few people have been prepared to say they think they saw such an exotic beast as a tiger or a lion and it is either natural modesty or the desire not to look totally stupid that has probably accounted for many of the sightings being described as more like a creature of puma size. That's still a pretty big cat.

On occasion big cats have escaped from captivity in this country but it is extremely unlikely that they would last long without being detected and recaptured or killed, especially in the intensely urbanised environs of London. In the case of the Central Line puma, we would have to say that if such a creature had managed to get onto the line, it would almost certainly have been electrocuted and killed within minutes when it touched the conductor rails. For that reason the ghost of a puma haunting the line in this vicinity is possibly somewhat more plausible than a real living puma.

VICTORIA TO PIMLICO

During the building of the Victoria Line southwards from Victoria towards Brixton, an extension which opened in 1971, what was described as a 'large black presence' was seen between Victoria and Pimlico. Explained by the 'experts' as being a mist caused by changes in air pressure in the humid atmosphere of the subterranean workings, whatever it actually was proved sufficiently menacing to cause two of the tunnelling workers to drop their tools and rush away, swearing never to have anything more to do with building tube lines under London.

WATFORD TUNNEL

Between the present-day Watford Junction and King's Langley Stations on the West Coast Main Line are the Watford tunnels. One accommodates trains on the up and down fast lines; the slow lines run through the other. The line through the tunnels was opened in 1837 by the London & Birmingham Railway.

When the tunnels were being built, the workings unexpectedly penetrated part of a churchyard. Coffins were exposed and human remains in the form of bones rained down on the men engaged in the construction work, much to their horror. This desecration of the dead caused something of a scandal at the time.

As far as railwaymen were concerned, it also put a jinx on the tunnel and this part of the line. A number of nasty blowbacks occurred on the footplates of steam locomotives working through the tunnels. A blowback is a blast of fire which bursts out of the firebox into the cab and usually happens when a steam locomotive enters a tunnel at some speed and the driver has omitted to take the necessary steps to prevent it. Blowbacks have been known to cause serious, even fatal injuries to the men on the footplate.

Several of these blowbacks occurred, supposedly at the spot in the tunnel that was reckoned to be directly under the churchyard. It was easy, therefore, almost natural you might say, for the idea to emerge that the blowbacks were the work of the malevolent and indignant spirits of people whose remains had been disturbed during the building of the tunnels. This, of course, was their way of wreaking revenge on the living.

There have been no reports of blowbacks in the Watford tunnels for many years. This is not surprising given that diesel and electric traction units have no fireboxes.

8

THE HAUNTED UNDERGROUND IN FILM, TELEVISION AND BOOKS

SOUTH KENTISH TOWN

In the short story, *South Kentish Town*, broadcast on BBC radio (9 January 1951), Sir John Betjeman (1906-1984) tells of a clerk who mistakenly gets off an Underground train when the doors accidentally open at a disused station. The train then drives off leaving the man standing there alone. Confused, he decides to climb the spiral staircase, all 294 steps. As he nears the top he bangs his head on the floorboards of one of the shops above the station. He calls out but no one hears him. The man then descends back down to the platform.

It is a wonderful eerie story and is well worth the read. It evokes a terrifying feeling of being trapped as well as the fear of not knowing how to escape from an awful predicament. Reputedly based on a true account of a man who alighted on South Kentish Town Station in 1924, shortly after it was closed (although he quickly got back onto the train), the story reflects the way in which the London Underground has proved to be a fertile location for atmospheric and supernatural settings. Betjeman's tale taps into our fears of the dark and of being alone with untold possibilities of nasty things lurking, particularly in the bowels of this labyrinthine network.

Not only has the London Underground featured in many short stories and novels it has also been used in many films and television productions. Not all have been about hauntings or the supernatural. Although this genre has been represented in a number of productions it is surprising that there has not been more made of this location given its creepy atmosphere. Transport for London are accommodating and have welcomed many film companies to use their facilities although some companies have found it more economical to shoot from a mock-up studio. Nonetheless the theme set out in Betjeman's short story of a lone commuter has provided plenty of material for variations on this theme, although some of these have been much less subtle than *South Kentish Town*. Whilst the terrors of Betjeman's unfortunate clerk were mainly in his own mind, other characterisations set on the Underground have produced more sinister phantoms and creatures who threaten those who dare to be alone.

Right: Sir John Betjeman (1906–1984), poet and author of the atmospheric *South Kentish Town*. His statue was fittingly unveiled at the reopening of St Pancras International Station in November 2007.

Below: The disused South Kentish Town Station (1907-1924) which stands adorned with advertising boards and signs and is now (June 2008) used as a cash converters and a sauna and massage business.

QUATERMASS AND THE PIT

One of the great BBC Television series was Nigel Kneale's *Quatermass and the Pit,* broadcast in the winter of 1958-1959. It managed successfully to scare audiences up and down the country with a younger generation (and some older ones) cowering behind the armchair to watch it. It was a retelling of a ghost story in which a scientific event leads to the explanation of supernatural phenomena. The main setting for the television series was a studio-constructed building site whereas the film version (1967) was set mainly around a fictional Underground station, 'Hobbs End'. During the extension of what was supposed to be the Victoria Line, workers discover what they believe to be an unexploded Second World War bomb near the station platform. As they gradually begin to uncover the mysterious object it turns out to be a spaceship, millions of years old, bearing the fossilised bodies of dead aliens. Professor Bernard Quatermass, an unconventional scientist, is brought in to shed light on this disturbing discovery which turns out to have unforeseen effects on the local populace. Quatermass discovers that people living in the area have experienced ghostly manifestations and poltergeist outbreaks since the building of 'Hobbs End' Underground station in 1927. The fictional station is located at the end of a road called Hobbs Lane. A scene from the film shows Quatermass looking at two street signs. The older sign is spelt Hob's End about which Quatermass is informed, 'that's an old name for the Devil'.

Quatermass and the Pit weaves all the ingredients of a supernatural story: aliens, superstition, archaeological excavation, possession, haunted houses, science, ghosts and horror. Despite the importance of the Underground to the story, the film (known as *5 Million Miles from Earth* in the US) was shot mainly at Ealing Studios. The changing of the set from a building site on the television series to an Underground station for the film was an inspired one. Construction of the actual Victoria Line started in the early 1960s, some five years before the film. When the line was extended south of the Thames to Brixton the engineers encountered various problems, including the finding of fossils and a number of human remains from an old plague pit. The disruption to the pit soon prompted reports of a ghostly presence haunting the area.

NEVERWHERE

Neverwhere was a six-part television serial first shown in 1996. Based on the book by Neil Gaiman, it tells the macabre tale of a sinister world known as 'London Below'. Set in modern-day London (London Above) the series uses the Underground to reflect an uncongenial city that has been left behind. The central character, Richard Mayhew, an average sort of man, stumbles into the murky world of London Below which consists of a city of monsters, murderers, monks and angels. Familiar names take on a new significance in London Below. The Angel, Islington is a real angel, the Black Friars are dark priests, and Old Bailey is a character who wears clothing made of feathers.

The closed Down Street Station, which was converted for use as a secret command centre during the Second World War, was used for the banquet scene in the serial.

Façade of former Down Street Station on the Piccadilly Line, closed in 1932. Tucked away as it was in a side street off Piccadilly and close to the adjacent stations of Green Park (originally Dover Street) and Hyde Park Corner, it is a mystery as to why this station was ever built. What lurks behind these carefully secured doors?

TROGLODYTES!

The idea of people or creatures living in the Underground over many years has not only been the stuff of urban legend but has also provided the inspiration for some films. These myths have varied from large rodents and hybrid creatures to a forgotten troglodytic race whose ranks have been added to by vagabonds, escaped prisoners and people hiding during the Blitz who never returned to the surface. Such accounts suggest that these subterranean survivors have been reduced to near-bestial form according to *Fortean Times* reporter Michael Goss:

> They [allegedly] prowl the sewers and railway tunnels showing themselves as little as possible …
> They probably eat the sandwiches and burgers we discard and it is 'widely' believed that they also
> eat tramps, drunks and other isolated late-night commuters.

On a more realistic note, Stephen Halliday in his book, *Underground to Everywhere* (2001), noted that Mass Observation (the social research organisation founded in 1937) reported in April 1943 on a study of tube life. They commented that some families had 'established themselves permanently in the shelters, having abandoned their homes altogether. Children almost three years old had never spent a night at home ...'. Halliday adds that 'this was the troglodytic mentality that the government had feared but it was confined to about 6,000 people'.

CREEP

The British horror film *Creep* (released 2005) focuses on a young woman, Kate, who, having failed to catch a taxi, heads for the Underground where she waits for a train. Seemingly trapped in the depths of the Underground she falls asleep (supposedly at Charing Cross). When she awakes she is alone and begins to panic until a train pulls in. As Kate realizes she is the only passenger the train stops in the tunnel and the lights goes out. Her nightmares are just about to start. She eventually meets up with a couple who have made their home in a small room at the station. The man jokingly tells Kate about a creature creeping around killing homeless people. Unfortunately this myth becomes an awful reality for Kate when she eventually encounters the 'creep', a mentally deranged cannibalistic hermit who feeds on strays and workers alone in the Underground. A poster for the film, which shows the bloody hand of a murdered passenger on an Underground train, was banned from all subway stations because it was deemed 'too gory'.

DEATH LINE

Creep owes a debt to an earlier film, *Death Line* (1972 aka *Raw Meat*), starring Donald Pleasance. The film takes up the theme of a lost tribe of people, this time the descendants of workers (men and women) who were buried by a railway tunnel cave-in in 1895 during the excavation of a line between Holborn and Russell Square. Although abandoned they have survived and bred for many years by eating lone people who have ventured into the rabbit warren of tunnels. However, only one of the tribe is now alive and he is in search of new victims. When the body of a prominent Ministry of Defence official is found in Russell Square Station, a Scotland Yard inspector is called in to investigate. Before long his search uncovers a secret enclave of survivors beneath the tunnels.

AMERICAN WEREWOLF IN LONDON

Once again following the theme of a lone passenger, a scene in *American Werewolf in London* (1981) shows an unfortunate commuter getting off a train onto an empty 'Tottenham Court Road' platform. As he makes his way to the exit and then the escalator – still alone – he is stalked by the lurking presence of a werewolf. The man desperately runs to get away from the creature but soon falls prey to the beast.

REIGN OF FIRE

Another mythical creature, a dragon, is depicted in *Reign of Fire* (2002). During the extension of the 'Docklands Extension Line' (effectively a mock studio set) a huge hibernating dragon, asleep for hundreds of years, is discovered. The discovery unleashes the dragon, which then proceeds

Escalator at Canary Wharf Tube Station. The location was used for the film *28 Days Later* (2002).

to incinerate the construction workers with its fiery breath. Once released it then breeds at a phenomenal rate, eventually wiping out most of the world by 2024.

Apocalyptic and dystopian style films have also made use of the Underground such as *28 Days Later* (2002 – 'Canary Wharf'); *28 Weeks Later* (2007 – the actual exterior of the Jubilee line platform); *Survivors – The Lights of London parts 1 & 2* (1977); and *Code 46* (2004 – Canary Wharf). In a very different mould the British comedy *Bulldog Jack* (1935) made use of a fictitious 'secret' tunnel from a station called Bloomsbury to the Egyptian Room at the British Museum. Whilst this was a stage set the story was based on the ghost story of British Museum (see Underground Stations section).

TUBE TALES

A more subtle approach is taken in the film *Tube Tales* (1999) which follows a series of mysterious and funny encounters, based on the true-life experiences of London Underground passengers. The nine stories unfold against a background of trains, corridors and escalators. One of the stories, *Steal Away*, follows two young people escaping from a robbery that they have committed. Using Holborn and Aldwych Stations as locations they try to escape and find themselves on what appears to be a disused station until a mysterious train pulls up and they board. Although the young man was shot during the robbery he appears to have escaped unscathed – or has he?

Other television series with a supernatural element featured on the Underground include *Doctor Who – The Dalek Invasion of the Earth* (1964) which made extensive use of the derelict 'Wood Lane' station; *The Web of Fear* (1968) – several scenes were shot in the Greenwich Foot Tunnel but the film-makers mainly used a studio set; *The Chase* (1965); *Mysterious Planet* (1986 –an underground civilisation is discovered under Marble Arch Station); and *White City*; *The Sun Makers* (1977) at Camden Town. Other sci-fi series include *Blakes 7: Ultraworld* (1980) and more recently *Primeval* (2007). The *Primeval* episode, as with almost all filming locations beneath the London Underground, was filmed at Aldwych.

The use of disused stations as locations is limited for health and safety reasons, now making Aldwych the only disused station in which filming is allowed. Aldwych has also been the location for spooky films such as *Death Line* (1972), *Ghost Story* (1974), *Creep* (2004) and the television series *Most Haunted*, which chose the station in September 2002 to locate any ghosts that might be haunting the station. *Lifeforce* (1985 at Chancery Lane) also deals with alien forces taking possession of London although this time turning the population into zombies.

The most interesting documentary to be made about hauntings was *Ghosts of the Underground* which was shown on Channel 5 in October 2006. Drawing largely on the experiences of people who had spent most of their working lives on the Underground, many of the accounts were authentic as well as chilling. The programme did not sensationalise but allowed a number of men to talk about their experiences of phenomena they could not explain. Some of them admitted to not believing in ghosts but acknowledged how very scared they were by what they had seen or heard. This rather understated approach not only brought a quality of eeriness to the programme but also made the accounts sound very believable.

LITERATURE

As with film and television the London Underground has provided the setting for many novels and short stories. There are books that deal with dark themes set under London such as Clare Clark's murder story, *The Great Stink* (Viking, 2005). This evokes the smells, filth, rats, and the untold detritus that assemble in the sewerage tunnels of London just prior to the building of the London Underground. However, compared with films, books about hauntings are thinner on the ground which is surprising given the ominous and eerie subterranean setting of parts of the Underground.

Sir Thomas Graham Jackson (1835-1924) was a leading architect as well as a writer of ghost stories. In the short story, *A Romance of the Piccadilly Tube*, he created one of the first ghost stories set in the London Underground. The central character, George Markham, catches a crowded train at Piccadilly Station where he later witnesses a very grisly accident involving a man he knows who is swept under a passing train. A commuter nightmare is the theme in the short story by R. Chetwynd-Hayes, *Non-Paying Passengers* (1974). The main character, Percy Fortesque, sees the ghost of his despised late wife, Doris, reflected in a train window. Later, his in-laws are doomed to haunt the London Underground for all eternity. In one of his last ghost stories, *Bad Company* (1956), Walter De La Mare opens with the chilling line, 'It is very seldom that one encounters evil in a human face …'. The story opens with the narrator descending one of London's 'many subterranean railway stations.' He describes the eeriness of the platform with its 'glare and glitter, the noise, the very air one breathes affect nerves and spirits. One expects vaguely strange meetings in such surroundings. On this occasion, the expectation was justified.' The story unfolds when the man boards the train and sits next to a cadaverous-looking old man whose appearance made the narrator

The old Aldgate East station was demolished and its platform space used for the new tracks – all, that is, except for the extra space set back for the staircase on the eastbound platform. This is the view from a passing train. (© Pendar Sillwood)

recoil in disgust. The haunting figure continues to lure the man to a decrepit London residence in order to reveal a last will and testament.

A variation on the theme set out in *Death Line* is *London Revenant* (2006) by Conrad Williams which deals with another kind of lost soul. These are the drop-outs who haunt the Underground but among them lurks the 'Pusher' whose pleasure is to push people under trains as well as torturing people who live above ground. Another novel which takes the combination of the Underground and a sinister presence is Tobias Hill's *Underground* (Faber, 2000), which takes the reader down long-lost tunnels, makeshift passages, locked and forgotten stations in search of grisly murders. Nicholas Royle's *The Director's Cut* (2000) concerns a psychotic film maker who finds shelter in a dead station whilst murdering passengers on the tube.

The London Underground has provided a great backcloth for eerie stories. For many people, notably those working on the Underground, it has been the source of unusual and unexplained experiences. If you find yourself alone on a platform, in a carriage or a corridor of one of the stations mentioned in this book you might have cause to reflect on what you have read. If you happen to be on the receiving end of a 'supernatural' experience then … well, at least let us know. We would be interested to hear.

Other local titles published by The History Press

Haunted London

JAMES CLARK

From the monk ghost who clanks his chains on Buckingham Palace's terrace every Christmas Day to the phantom horse-bus that occasionally rattles along Bayswater Road, the colourful tales featured here create a scary selection of ghostly goings-on that will captivate anyone interested in the supernatural history of London.

978 0 7524 4459 8

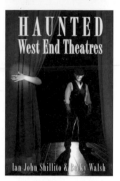

Haunted West End Theatres

IAN SHILLITO AND BECKY WALSH

In researching these theatrical ghost stories, the first time a collection of this magnitude has been put together, the authors have held vigils in dark auditoriums, lonely stairwells and melancholy boxes, behind the scenery and underneath the stages in the search for theatrical phantoms. From the Lyceum to the Lyric, the astounding results demonstrate the historical links between spirits and the stage.

978 0 7524 4521 2

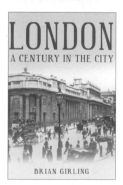

Haunted Wandsworth

JAMES CLARK

This collection contains both well-known and hitherto unpublished tales of the ghosts, mysteries and legends of Wandsworth. The chilling selection includes the infamous Victorian murder mystery of Charles Bravo, poisoned one April night and still haunting the room in which he died, and the 'Poltergeist Girl of Battersea'. These scary stories will captivate anyone interested in the supernatural history of the area.

978 0 7524 4070 5

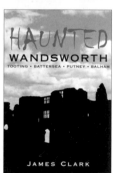

London A Century in the City

BRIAN GIRLING

Utilising rare and unseen photographs, the book offers an exploration and celebration of the City of London through a century from the 1850s to the 1960s. It is enhanced by a colour section featuring very rare early colourtint and oilette postcards, many of which show uncommon views of the City. This book will revive a half-forgotten memory or reveal times we never knew in a city which is known and loved worldwide.

978 0 7524 4507 6

If you are interested in purchasing other books published by The History Press, or in case you have difficulty finding any History Press books in your local bookshop, you can also place orders directly through our website
www.thehistorypress.co.uk